LIFE AFTER WORK

LIFE AFTER WORK

THE ARRIVAL OF
THE AGELESS SOCIETY

———————◆◆◆———————

Michael Young and Tom Schuller

(with Johnston Birchall and Gwyneth Vernon)

HarperCollins
An Imprint of HarperCollins*Publishers*

First published in 1991 by
HarperCollins Publishers,
77–85 Fulham Palace Road,
Hammersmith, London W6 8JB

9 8 7 6 5 4 3 2 1

BRITISH LIBRARY CATALOGUING IN PUBLICATION DATA

Young, Michael
Life After Work
1. England. Retirement
I. Title   II. Schuller, Tom
306.380942

ISBN 0–00–215929–5

Phototypeset in Linotron Sabon by
Input Typesetting Ltd, London

Printed and bound in Great Britain by
HarperCollins Book Manufacturing, Glasgow

TO SUE CHISHOLM, JOHANNE SCHULLER
AND WYN TUCKER

Contents

Acknowledgements

Our debts are numerous. The first is to the Leverhulme Trust for its generous support, and particularly to Ronald Tress, former Director of the Trust, for suggesting our partnership in the first instance.

The book's gestation period has been long and several people contributed to it. Johnston Birchall worked almost full-time on the project for more than two years, interviewing, organising the material and analysing the main survey. He also helped in the development of our thinking about the structure of time. Gwyneth Vernon joined us towards the end of the project, and helped greatly in drawing together the threads. Diana Robbins carried out the fieldwork for the hospital study.

The problem of identifying the people with whom we wished to talk was solved with the help initially of Professor P.M. Higgins, the Professor of Community Medicine at Guy's Hospital. Margaret Jones, Muriel Kerr and Margery Thorne assisted in the piloting of the survey, Claire Nissel in carrying out the interviews. Libby Birchall not only conducted many of the interviews but also played a significant part in the organisation of the data over a considerable period. Ian Cullen responded generously to an assortment of requests for technical assistance. Lesley Cullen carried out the checking of material with customary efficiency.

We are grateful too to Peter Willmott, Nick Bosanquet, Sally Greengross, Margot Jefferys, Peter Laslett, Janet Atfield, Michael Fogarty, John Saville, Roger Warren Evans and to Jo Anne Robertson, our editor, for their comments.

Sasha Young gave us great help in the organisation and editing of the book.

As always, a special debt is owed to Sue Chisholm and Wyn

Tucker at the Institute of Community Studies for their unfailing support.

Without the generous gift of time from all those interviewed and from George Davies and Trevor Franklin at Fords, the book could not of course have been written.

ONE

The New Prospects for Retirement

'Seventy is younger now than it was
yesterday.'   *Mrs Barker, Plumstead*

Schoolchildren tumbling over each other in their playgrounds
are the more obvious harbingers of the future. Revolutionaries
amongst them could still be alive in the second half of the
next century even if their zeal has diminished a little by then. We
are looking for the future in a more unlikely direction, to older
men and women some of whom will not see out *this* century.
Will they follow the warriors who have struggled against sex-
discrimination by reacting more and more strongly against
age-discrimination?

They have numbers on their side, in themselves witness to the
great social achievement of this century in adding twenty-five
years to the expectation of life. 'Our earthly time allowance has
rapidly shot up'*: the possibilities of human life are not so often
extinguished by people dying before their allotted time. There
are more old people and, owing to the decline in fertility, they
bulk larger in the population. Old age could once be regarded
as a sort of terminal illness; it cannot any longer.

But the extension of life has only been one of a series of
transformations which have created a new class system made up
of age-classes alongside the common-or-garden social classes. As
a result of the changes that have occurred in the situation of the
old and, for similar reasons, of the young, modern society in all
parts of the world where industrialisation has held sway has
become rigidly age-stratified.

The social history of Britain which pioneered the new industry
has in one variation or another been followed almost every-

* R. Blythe, *The View in Winter*, p.11. The full references for publications are
in the Select Bibliography at the end of the book.

where, from the United States to Germany, from France to Japan, with the new order being wrenched out, time and time again, from the bosom of the family. Pre-industrial society rested on this single ancient institution which, for millennia, had an all-embracing sweep, performing all functions and straddling all ages. The family produced its own food and clothing, educated its children, sustained its old and controlled its members so that they served these ends. The family was the great generalist, as with a much reduced role it still is.

The new age-locked society has been made possible by the gains in productivity which industry has brought about. When the family was both economy and society it had one great disadvantage: domestic production did not yield much more than a basic living. Before the coming of industry men, women and children had to work from almost the cradle to almost the grave because they were at the margin of subsistence. There was little or no room for people of any age who could not grow and rear the food they ate and make the goods they consumed. Almost every consumer (outside the landowning classes) had to be a producer as well. Who would not toil, should not eat. Death limited the growth of population and people of any age had to work up to the limits of their capacity as soon as, and as long as, they had any capacity to offer.*

For the old, this meant until they dropped. 'The time to retire', said William Randolph Hearst, 'is when God retires you.' In the Middle Ages there was hardly any old age beyond work. So also with the young. Before industrialisation boys and girls no longer infants were considered little adults,** dressed up like them, and

---

* Although it never went as far as in Inca society where 'Judges, called ilacta-mayu, would walk into the houses and check that everyone was engaged in useful work; the blind, the lame, the deaf and dumb, all had their tasks to accomplish, according to their capacity.' G. Minois, *History of Old Age, From Antiquity to the Renaissance*, p.13.
** Biology obviously imposes some limits upon development. 'Adults in authority can to some extent impose their conceptions of childishness both on children and sometimes on other adults too. In this sense the whole concept of childhood could be said to be a man-made phenomenon. Thus childhood may be lengthened and prolonged at some periods of history, and abbreviated at others, according to adult perceptions, needs and expectations. Even so, while any individual can be kept back or indeed hastened on in his social

2

in farming families almost as soon as they could toddle were sent off to work in the fields, gleaning the corn or scaring off the birds. Girls were set to help their mothers prepare food, fetch water, watch over the small animals around the house and make things out of the wool, skins, clay and wood from their holding, if the family was fortunate enough to have one. The work of children was necessary – so for the support of their families the more the offspring, the better. They were not accorded the rights of adults but only the duties. So work it was, non-specialist work often calling on a range of skills, with precious little time for play and with most of their education coming from their parents or older siblings. For Daniel Defoe it was a sign that all was well with the state of eighteenth century England when

> If we knock'd at the Door of any of the master manufac-
> turers, we presently saw a house full of lusty fellows, some
> at the dye-vat, some dressing the clothes, some at the
> loom . . . the women and children of whom are always busy
> carding, spinning etc. so that no hands being unemploy'd
> all can gain their bread, even from the youngest to the
> ancient; hardly anything above four years old but its hands
> are sufficient to itself.*

Separating off the ages

It was the factory that put an end to the all-age family as the unit of production and brought into existence age-classes where there had been none before. The gains in productivity brought about by the factories and the associated agricultural and other improvements allowed masses of people, for the first time in human history, to live above the subsistence level. But the fact of there being gains did not in itself dictate the manner in which

---

development by the surroundings in which he lives, there are some limits to the speed at which most children can become socialised into adult ways.' N. Tucker, *What is a Child?*, pp.26–7.
* D. Defoe, *A Tour through Great Britain* (London: G. Strahan, 1727), vol.III, p.101.

they should be distributed. The surplus above subsistence was not used as it would have been if the family had remained the altogether dominant institution. For then the extra productivity might well have been used, not, as it was in practice, to relieve the old and the young from the obligation to contribute to their own upkeep, but to spread the benefits of extra leisure and income across all age groups, without any of them being required to give up work entirely. The world would have had a different notion of full employment from the one that has been adopted. Full employment would have been in existence wherever children started work early, as they had done before, and older people continued to work late, as they had done before, so that people of all ages would have been doing paid work but with ever decreasing hours for all of them. Leisure would have been spread around evenly instead of being so heavily concentrated at each end of the age spectrum. Everyone of any age could have had time for education just as everyone would have had to spend time on work. Consumers and producers would have remained the same people, and no new age-classes created of consumers who were not allowed to be producers. This is all now a might-have-been but not necessarily a will-never-be; the might-have-been could be revived in a new form in the future. We will come back to the possibility in the final chapter.

The option was never weighed up and then, after proper reflection, rejected. If it had been, the subsequent history of the industrial world, without schools confined to children and without children and old people being excluded from work, would have been so different as hardly to be imaginable. As it is, the family as the generalist has given way to industry as the specialist. Specialisation has been demanded by the growth of an ever more complex economy and, as it turns out, of an ever-more fragmented society. The globe has been pulled together into one network by specialised communications but pulled apart by new and equally specialised institutions for industry and education, health and amusement, which have taken over what the family, as an all-age affair, once did largely on its own.*

* The trend was already identified much earlier this century, for instance in the Report of the President's Research Committee on Social Trends, com-

The reduction of the family's productive role has had a marked effect on incentives. Industry has always needed workers who want more goods and services and want them insatiably. If workers had ever been satisfied with what they had, industrial discipline would have disappeared. This fear about what was going to keep men at work if their 'needs' could be satisfied with less exertion was very much alive in the early days of the industrial revolution. Thomas Malthus voiced it in 1798.

> The main part of the question respecting the wants of mankind, relates to their power of calling forth the exertions necessary to acquire the means of expenditure. It is unquestionably true that wealth produces wants; but it is a still more important truth, that wants produce wealth. Each cause acts and reacts upon the other, but the order, both of precedence and of importance is with the wants which stimulate to industry.*

He was followed by many people of similar mind who lamented the unfortunate fact that so many workers eased off when they had earned enough to satisfy their needs. St Monday (as it was called in the nineteenth century) was for long to all those who did not observe its rule a ridiculous, even monstrous residue which had survived from medieval saints' days: St Monday enticed workers too easily satisfied with their pay into taking off an entire day when they should have been obediently at work.** They needed a more driving acquisitiveness to spur them on.

The situation would have been still more worrying if children and older people had remained bread-winners as well as bread-eaters. As it was, their gradual removal from the labour force meant that workers had more dependants, more people to work

---

missioned by Herbert Hoover. William Ogburn concluded that what was happening was a 'greater individualization of the family'. It had yielded to outside agencies its traditional economic, protective, educational and entertainment functions. William F. Ogburn, with Clark Tibbins, 'The Family and Its Functions', in *Recent Trends in the United States*. p.663.
* T.R. Malthus, *Principles of Political Economy*, pp.469–70.
** E.P. Thompson, 'Time, Work, Discipline and Industrial Capitalism', p.74.

for, more needs that had to be satisfied. Their altruism made workers into work-horses.

The removal of the young and the old from the labour force also strengthened incentives in another way. If they had not been removed, increasing leisure would have been spread around all ages instead of being concentrated on young and old. People neither young nor old but in-between would then have not only had more leisure but more leisure than they wanted or knew what to do with. They would have had to grapple with the 'problem' of leisure. As Henry Durant said much later,

> The difficulties and perplexities arising from a greater number of persons than ever before having means and energy at their disposal to utilize during their free hours, are engaging the attention of educationalists, social workers and all those whose business it is to attend to the working of society.*

Part of the fear of those whose business is business was that, if their employees had too much free time, work would cease to be salient in their lives. It would not dominate their time, and then they would cease to be so devoted to it. This fear has never been entirely extinguished but at least there is much less cause for it than there would have been if those with the least clout, the old and the young, had not been prevented from working.

The rise of the State

The role of the new nation state in the whole transformation was crucial. The family did not give up its functions willingly: it fought strongly against the take-over. The tenant farmers held out against enclosure of their lands; the families dependent upon the domestic handicrafts all over Britain put up trenchant opposition to the new machines even when they did not go so far as to join the Luddites; after education was made compulsory in

---

* H. Durant, *The Problem of Leisure*, pp.2–3.

1870 some poor parents rioted against the new schools which were going to take their children and their children's labour away from them.* In all phases of the long struggle the State was engaged on the other side, harnessing its sovereign force and its money to put down the traditional comprehensive family and subtract from it some of its more crucial functions, or (as in education) force itself on the family as a partner. Though always in the name of reform and always to demonstrate a perfectly genuine benevolence for the interests of the young and the old, the State appropriated some of the main roles of the family. It weakened the family's own basic framework for distributing its resources between all its members according to their needs and challenged its mini-collectivist sentiments with an individualism more in tune with the exigencies of industry. The fulcrum of modern society has been the alliance between the State and industry. The consequences of the State's victory, particularly for the upbringing of children, are still unwinding through the social structure centuries later.

Meanwhile the old had to be prevailed upon to withdraw from the labour market. They had to recognise that to 'retire', once their duty to avoid, had now become their duty to honour. Eventually common parlance had to give retirement its new meaning and its new respectability. None of this would have been done without the State. Characteristically, it was the civil service that invented retirement in its modern form and tied it down to specific ages.** The civil service extended the practice in 1859 and, later in that century, fixed on sixty as the age when

---

* 'The new board schools were built in the slums, but the people were not at all grateful; in fact they rose up in their wrath at this interference with their liberty. To be forced to send their children to school was too much, so they chased away the unfortunate builders, who had to be given police protection while building.' M. and C.B.B. Quennell, *History of Everyday Things in England*, vol.IV, p.127. The new law was of course disregarded. In the Suffolk village of Akenfield the school's log book recorded that in 1889, 'There is now a Night School for the children who must work in the day-time' and in 1890: 'April 23rd. Field-work, gathering stones, cow-keeping and farmwork has reduced the average. 35 out of 61 attended. It is impossible, in my opinion, to teach either Geography or Grammar owing to the bad attendances caused by the farmers sending the children out on the fields'. R. Blythe, *Akenfield*, p.143.
** L. Hannah, *Inventing Retirement*, p.9.

7

people had to retire whether or not they wanted to and whether or not they were capable of carrying on: it was claimed that at that precise age 'bodily and mental vigour begin to decline'.* It would not have been any more sensible to say that at that age grey hair excludes grey matter. Compulsion was brought in to enforce retirement just as it was put behind education in its modern form. Since then policy (always backed by the rigours of the law) has lurched from one shaky rationalisation to another, with seventy being fixed as the qualifying age for a non-contributory pension in 1909, and sixty-five for a contributory pension in 1925.** The practice became still more ridiculous in 1940 when the retirement age for women was settled at sixty, five years younger than for the husbands whom they usually outlived, and still outlive, by a handsome margin.

As with the old so with the young. The child labour laws were the response to a great deal of valiant campaigning by a distinguished body of reformers but it was the State that introduced them and provided the sanctions against defaulters. The same thing happened with education: once again the reformers, in this case with the different churches to the fore, took the initiative, but without the State, and State money to make education free, the schools would have been patchy instead of having the complete coverage that they eventually did after education was made compulsory. From that time on, the new duty of childhood, to attend on unpaid work in the schoolhouse and to avoid paid work outside it, was recognised and enforced by the State. A new stage of life was thereby legislated. This did not of course mean that children, even if they had some adult duties, had adult rights any more than they had before schools were established so widely. They had to submit to a discipline which

---

* J. Jolly, S. Creigh and A. Mingay, *Age as a Factor in Employment*, p.111.
** In the United States the story was similar when the age threshold for retirement was set by the 1934 Social Security Act. 'No Senate or House committee requested a justification of age sixty-five, and the House voted down those few amendments from the floor that attempted to reduce the age for old-age assistance to sixty. Though in all probability neither gerontologists nor politicians expected that Social Security would rigidify the definition and isolation of old age, the facile acceptance of age sixty-five created momentous consequences.' H. Chudacoff, *How Old Are You?*, p.116.

could be even harsher than that undergone by their parents in their places of employment. If they were like adults at all they were adults writ small, sometimes very small. But if one had to put a date on the emergence of the new system of age classes (using the word in a rather different sense from that which applies to schools) 1870 would be as good a one as any.*

Thus it has been laid down that people's life-cycles should be cut into the standard segments we know today. The State has used its compulsory powers to decree that when they pass one birthday they have to enter school and at another leave the workforce, and, historically, employers have aped the State. In this respect people have been turned into numbers and the galaxy of differences between individuals deliberately ignored. When the clock strikes sixty-five, the magic wand of the State turns not coachmen into mice but men into old men or, when it strikes sixteen, pupils into workers. No transition. When the wand is waved millions of people have at once to obey. The power stems from the compulsory registration of everyone's dates of birth, marriage and death. Without ages being registered, as Napoleon long ago recognised, there could be no conscription for war; and we would have been without the rigid separation of the young and old which hardly seems rigid at all, we have become so accustomed to it.

The resulting age-stratification resembles a caste society in which people are born into a caste – peasants, merchants, nobility – in which they have to remain throughout their lives. Instead of birth, what counts in an industrial society is birth-date. Your birth-date determines thereafter much of what you *are*, and can *do*, at different stages of your life. The feudal overlord of this temporal caste system is the State. It has laid down a national curriculum which lasts for life. By doing so it

---

* 'By the 1870s, formally structured age-gradings had become introduced throughout the United States. Though compulsory attendance laws had not yet taken root, in 1870 the proportion of white children ages five to seventeen who attended school exceeded 61 per cent, up from 35 per cent in 1830 and 50 per cent in 1850. Graded classes now locked a significant proportion of American children into age-determined groupings and engendered in adults the assumption that these groupings were endemic to the educational experience.' H. Chudacoff, *How Old Are You?*, p.36.

has by a circular process created the dependants who have provided the justification for its own existence. The State has taken on a welfare role which has made it a welfare state, with the function of financing and controlling many millions of people who are not permitted a livelihood. But one argument in this book is that the overlordship is now being threatened by the extraordinary expansion of the same age-classes at each end of life. We hope it is a safe prediction that the State will not be allowed for very much longer to appear as the uninvited but still in a way the presiding godfather at every birthday party.

The two extreme age-classes have been swollen out by a series of steps, each of them peculiar to the one or the other. The elongation of retirement has followed on the improvements in health. Better health is one of the results of a higher standard of life when this has taken the form of more and better food and this has benefited those who used to eat too little, even if it has harmed those who eat too much; alongside this have come better sanitation and better housing; better medicine and better health care. Being more healthy, people live longer. But the retirement age has not been raised in line with the gain in life expectancy. If the gain had since 1940 been wholly used for extending working life, the standard retirement age would already be seventy and on the way up to seventy-five in 2025.* But as it is, with no such adjustment, the number of people in Britain entitled to draw a retirement pension has been rising steadily. The proportion of the population above pensionable age rose from 5 per cent in 1901 to 10.9 per cent in 1951 and 15 per cent in 1987; and even if it levels off temporarily, it is expected to shoot up again in the early part of the next century. The number of people over seventy-five is growing faster than any other age group. It has become less and less true that work-enders are also life-enders.

Superimposed on this major trend, common to all industrial societies, has been another of more recent origin which has been common to most – the practice of leaving work earlier. Men though not women have been ending their paid jobs a good deal

---

* Organisation for Economic Co-operation and Development, *Reforming Public Pensions*, p.79.

earlier than they used to. The practice was given an impetus by the slump of the early 1980s but survived strongly into the following boom and beyond. The government expects early retirement to stay.* The labour market has changed its shape, perhaps permanently, which means that to the growing numbers of people who are over the normal retirement age now have to be added the many who have retired below it.

The elongation for the old has been accompanied by a similar one for the young, this time more as a result of deliberate action by the State. The official age for leaving work has not been reduced but the official age for leaving school has been raised progressively, to fourteen, to fifteen, to sixteen. Each rise was hailed as a testament to progress and especially progress in an economy which needed (but did not necessarily get) ever better educated people if the country was to compete effectively with others. The rises in the official ages have been followed by a further expansion in the numbers staying on at school voluntarily and in the numbers of students continuing into higher education. The details vary; but the general drift, again, has been the same in all industrial countries. Whether education has to be so much confined to the young, or remain compulsory for so long, are other questions; but in some form education is clearly necessary to the kind of society we are in, and it will continue to be.

The health revolution has also affected young people. Partly as a result of better nutrition, the outcome has been almost as dramatic as for the old. While old age has been postponed, childhood has stopped earlier. For girls the general age of menarche has fallen from seventeen and more a century ago to about thirteen; and of puberty in boys by almost as much, although not as far. Children of twelve and thirteen are so much taller and more robust that older people do not give themselves away so much by saying how young policemen look as by saying how old schoolchildren look. The tension is that on the one hand childhood as an administrative category has been expanding as

---

* *Employment Gazette*, March 1988, pp.124–5. Quoted by N. Bosanquet in his evidence to the House of Commons Employment Committee, *The Employment Patterns of the Over 50s*, Vol.2, p.24.

a matter of government policy while on the other, without any decision by anybody, childhood as a sexual and physical category has been contracting. But people who have come of age in one sense are still children in another; they are not acknowledged as political citizens until they are eighteen.

Class comparisons

The new age-classes, and around them the new class structure which has been created by the double series of cumulative changes we have been describing, are not unlike the ordinary social classes. Both kinds of class in their modern forms had their origins in the industrial revolution. The members of the two extreme age-classes are different in their chronological ages but not so different that they cannot be lumped together for their similarities, as young people who have not started work or older people who have finished it. The members of ordinary social classes are different too in many of their attributes – occupation primarily, but with wealth, power, education and housing playing a part – but still have enough in common to justify them being classed together. The three main age-classes can also be ranked in terms of the status attached to them, with the people of working age having the highest status and, we would say, the young coming next and the old coming last. Within each general age-class different statuses attach to people of various ages, the sixty-year-old as against the seventy-year-old, or the fourteen-year-old as against the ten, with the gradient being up for the young and down for the old. But the age-classes are not formed out of the occupational structure: their members do not have ordinary occupations – the result being that the young have not yet been caught up in the ordinary class structure and the old have to some extent left it behind. In many ways, rather than describing behaviour only in terms of the general inclusive system of social classes, it says more about people, and is also descriptive of their way of life, to consider them as starting in one age-class, then entering an occupational class, and ending in another age-class.

In another respect the age-classes and the main occupational

classes – that is, the working class, the middle class and so forth
– are alike: the boundaries of each have become more fuzzy.
People can be thought of, and think of themselves, as belonging
to a social class where their ranking on a series of different
criteria is more or less the same – the status attributed to them
for their income being similar to their status for their level of
education, their housing, their power, even their style of dress
and the type of their car. But their rankings on the different
scales are now not so often the same: more difficult to place in
the ordinary class system are people like businessmen who have
much money but little education or actors and parsons who are
the opposite. This is especially so for people who have started
life in one social class and then as a result of social mobility
moved into another.

The boundaries of the age-classes have also become more
blurred. The pensionable ages laid down by the State have
retained their immense influence. A majority of people still retire
at these official ages. But the trend we have just mentioned
towards earlier work-ending has been increasing the variability
of the leaving ages and will presumably do so still more in the
future, and people can now draw a State pension without having
to give up work. At the other end of the spectrum many youngsters involved in government training schemes have been paid
and have had work experience without being in ordinary
employment. They have been in some kind of half-way house
between education and work. Moreover, it is not just the age-
boundaries themselves that have become blurred. Older people
can in their own way be as trendy and almost as responsive to
fashion as the younger, and romance as much something for
them as for their grandchildren.

But for all that, the age-classes, if definable at the margin with
less precision, remain intact in so far as they comprise vast
sections of the population. Their members are mostly still charac-
terised by not being able to work – many of the people in their
fifties who have been sacked partly because of their age are
certainly like that – and, as a consequence, young and old are
dependent in whole or part on the State for their support, that
is for their pensions or other benefits or for the cost of their
education and (sometimes) a grant to go with it. The State

which played such a crucial part in bringing the age-classes into existence is still the prop, indeed the legislator, without which the two age-classes on which we are concentrating could not exist. The new age-class structure is therefore particularly open to challenge. What the State can do, the State can undo.

But it will not happen unless a further set of changes is set in motion to alter the culture in which the State operates. The State is both a strange abstraction and not an abstraction at all, providing as it does money, a mouthpiece, a legal procedure and a police-power which can be put to work for those who take control of it. The State is like the robe and the mask which people don in some other cultures, thus investing themselves with the authority of a shaman or medicine-man. But the wearers and weavers of the power act very largely in accord with the way others think they should, all accepting that age runs through the labyrinth of modern society like a guiding thread. Most people still believe as if in gospel that all children should be punctually at school between this age and that and older people retire at a set point.

A general obsession

The whole society is obsessed with age, well beyond the State. It is as if the compulsive game of age-stratification were being played in a dark room but people born into a particular cohort are more than ever expected to behave in important respects like other people born with the stamp of that same year upon them. Their parents give them their introductory but essential education when they compare them with their fellows of the same date, noticing they are bigger, or more advanced in their attainment of speech or hind-leg walking, or cleverer, or smaller, less advanced, less clever, in short more 'backward', than other infants of the same age. 'You're a big girl now, you should be able to tell the time.' It is dinned into them again when they are reaching a critical birthday that makes them eligible for a place in a crèche, a day nursery or a nursery school or reaching the age of five which propels them into the ordinary infant school along with all the others who are marching in step with them.

Children's most rigorous training in age standardisation starts then. From that time on they are lockstepped together with a lot of other unlikes in year-groups of five-year-olds which become six and seven and anything-year-olds. They sit with them and play with them and scream and moan, complain and rejoice with them, and develop the appropriate rituals and feelings of rivalry and envy, superiority and inferiority, for the other children who are climbing up the age-order of the school a year or two later or sooner. The children at the top of the school can seem almost 'grown up' to those who have just entered at the bottom and have not yet learnt the small distinctions in speech and manner between the ages, the distinctions which bulk so large to those learning the age-maze everyone has to learn on their route to adulthood.

When they leave school or university they are given no respite but can be plunged straight into the main age-order of the adult world which is continually propped up by what people learn to do before and after they are in that age-order. A career is a hierarchy of jobs, still predominantly a male affair but no less real for that, with a timetable attached so that people know full well what rank they should have reached when they are twenty-eight or thirty or thirty-six just as they know that if they have not reached a certain place in the hierarchy they may later on be considered 'too old' at forty or fifty for any job at all. If they are on the ladder but have failed to get advancement at the critical age, they can immediately calculate what is the highest level they can attain in twenty years' time as long as on their now more modest career path they do not falter again and are not too put down by the success of the high flyer who gets advancement before the usual age, the professor at twenty-eight, the tennis star at fifteen or the mathematical genius at twelve. In business, ambitious executives who are not put down go on reading the oracle of advancement until their 'career menopause', when they have glumly to accept that they have reached their peak. If they do not recognise they have reached it they do not deserve to have got as far as they have.

The arrangements foster anxious reflection on the few years that remain before the next critical stage, and before the eventual retirement and the eventual death. Such anxiety makes for good industrial discipline. If you get off this train you cannot board it again. The cult of age-measurement, a misplaced mutant of the measurement which is necessary in science and technology, can shrink a lifetime into a series of calculations.

Throughout, people have to learn one of the most refined skills of the calculating society – the art of age-averaging – which inscribes a finely drawn set of portraits in their minds of the way a person of sixteen, forty or sixty-six looks so that they can say immediately, being programmed to do so, that a person behaves and looks about sixteen or forty or sixty-six or, if they are told another person's registered age – 'She looks young for her age', or 'He looks older than that'. More important, the programmes also contain a large series of behavioural specifications not just for babies but for people of any age so that those who do not conform can be criticised for it and so that people can follow the internalised instructions about how they themselves should behave. They learn to acquire a social age-clock alongside their biological clocks; the social clock triggers the right sort of behaviour at the right tick of the tock.

The fault-lines in society

The expansion of the two age-classes at the extremes has been obscured by their failure to attest their own difference from others and their own common interests with each other. Their class-consciousness has not been raised to the point where in any numbers they call their lot into question. For the old the class struggle has been gentle; grey power is rarely manifest. So far it is only the young with their youth culture who have begun to stake out a claim to an independent identity. But the importance of the new class of the young, and still more of the old, has been partially hidden from view for the reason we have already given. They have not become distinctive classes because in so far as they have had an ideology it has not been that of a leisure-based class but has remained a work-based one. If work remains Adam's curse, it is not necessarily resented. Most of the young know that they are undergoing preparation for the station they will later on take up in the economy and most of the old know that their status derives from the station they did have in the economy while they still belonged to the ordinary class structure. The *Zeitgeist* of the two leisure classes has been dominated by work. They have not – or at least the old have not – yet developed any strong collective sense of identity around any different values of their own. The old – our main interest here – will not become a fully fledged age-class until they have created a way of life which is distinctive from that of the still-working classes.

We conducted the enquiry because we believe that the situation is changing rapidly. The age-classes could be subordinated to the other classes much more easily when they were relatively small than they can now that nearly half the population is in one or other of them, with numbers increasing every day. The social controls which maintain the dominance of the work ethic are still in force, and stem in part from the State; but they are no longer so effective. Social change always becomes predictable when fault-lines appear in society. The fault-lines arise from deep-lying inconsistencies. Our argument is that there is a growing inconsistency between the size of the age-classes and their subordination or, as on the whole we prefer to put it, between the profiles of biological and social change. The 'old' and the 'young' are terms that refer to biology but which no longer have firm biological underpinning. Though young people mature earlier and old people age later than they did, the institutional control exercised over them dates from a different period and is still much the same as it was. The control has become anachronistic. It treats some people who are adults in most meanings of the word as though they are still children, and others who are still as fit and energetic as ever as though they have passed over a date-line from which there can be no return. The object of our enquiry is to find out a little more about the fault-lines, and especially whether older people (or some of them) are beginning to find the way forward to a new age, in the double sense of that word, which is no longer centred on paid work.

The need for new terms

For our purpose the old term will not do. As we said earlier, the word retirement came into use in this context in the last century. We think it should in due course be retired to the obscurity from which it emerged. It was once appropriate enough. Retirement was a kind of postscript to work which only had to be defined negatively, because the period used to be short. The health and strength of many people who earned their living by manual labour, and most did, was largely exhausted by the time they had earned the short holiday they were given before the grave. The watch or clock that employers traditionally handed over to their retiring workers was a deceit. It symbolised the gift of the time that was now to be their own rather than the employers'. But the new owner was going to wear out long before the watch.

All that has changed. The message that comes with the farewell present (if there is one) can wish the recipient a long and happy retirement but, if it is to be a long one, retirement is no longer the right word for what is no longer the same experience. 'What do you do, Mrs Bull?' 'Oh, I'm retired now; I finished last year.' All right if it was last year. But five years on, ten, twenty, is Mrs Bull still to be no more than 'retired'? Leaving paid work is a momentous event in anyone's life, more so than leaving school and the parental home, but once a person has, should it continue to brand him or her so indelibly and for so long? Once it can be detached from work this whole stage of life cries out to be regarded in a different light, as something more positive, not derived from work in the way a pension is derived from the work that preceded it, but distinctively worthwhile in its own right.

The term we have used instead of retirement is 'third age'.* It refers to the phase which can now last for twenty, thirty, even forty years of active life after leaving work and which would in Britain alone account for some ten million people. The term is not ours but has the advantage, as Laslett has said, of being 'a term not already tarnished',** as many of the more usual words

---

* The term is further discussed in Appendix 1.
** P. Laslett, *A Fresh Map of Life*, p.3.

have become, even those with the most august parentage. Classifiers have never allowed ageing to be a continuous process. The almost irresistible temptation has been to chop it up and to make ages into stages. The later stages then become tainted. Aristotle made no bones about it: he proposed the straightforward threefold division, which has retained its authority, of growth, stasis and decline. Shakespeare embellished the decline in *As You Like It* when he figured his sixth stage of life by the lean and slippered pantaloon with spectacles on nose and the last by second childishness and mere oblivion, sans teeth, sans everything. Even when the notion of an explicit decline has been avoided, it is still implicit in a fourfold classification like that of the Venerable Bede into childhood, youth, maturity and old age, with old age standing in contrast to maturity.* But we doubt whether any of the three, Aristotle, Shakespeare or Bede, would have been content with their classification if they had been alive now, with people expecting to live as long as they now do.

The term we prefer is of French origin, as used in *Les Universités du Troisième Age*, and the clubs with the same name which proliferated in France in the 1970s and 1980s. It has infiltrated into English and gained some currency through the University of the Third Age which was started in the early 1980s. At the time of writing the British U3A has over a hundred branches. The new attitude which is called for by demography, if by nothing else, could be helped along by the new term as it takes its place in the progression described by Laslett: 'First comes an era of dependence, socialization, immaturity and education; second an era of independence, maturity and responsibility, of earning and of saving; third an era of personal fulfilment'.**

The staging is threefold, like Aristotle's, but with opportunity substituting for decline. Much dependency and poor health is induced by the general expectation that a long-drawn-out decline is natural, almost inevitable. As it is not the one, it is therefore not the other. It should become possible in the future for more and more people to ward off the diseases associated with old age so that more and more can avoid decline almost until the

* J.A. Burrow, *The Ages of Man*, p.32.
** Laslett, *A Fresh Map of Life*, p.4.

end. Before long it could cease to be a joke to say that the ideal is to die young at an advanced age. Certainly the goal of medical and much other research should be to cap the boon of a long life with that of a quick death. The short lives of the past were (before modern medicine) often finished off by a quick death. As we escape from one kind of brevity we do not want to lose the other kind.

The potential for fulfilment

'An era of personal fulfilment' sounds very hopeful, and it would be wholly unrealistic to suggest that this is what necessarily happens in the third age. We do not need any survey to produce older people who for a whole variety of reasons are thoroughly miserable. Such people are obviously not being fulfilled. So when we refer to the third age in this way, what we are emphasising is its potentiality rather than its actuality. We are thinking of older people as having a certain kind of freedom – a negative freedom from coercion – which they may or may not convert into another kind of freedom, the positive kind.* 'Freedom from' is contrasted with 'freedom for' and the particular 'freedom from' which is possessed by the age-class is freedom from work. Instead of catching the same train every morning and strap-hanging to the same little desk, people can go fishing, read, dig the garden or do anything else that they could not do while bound into the daily round of work.

But what if they don't? Many of the people we interviewed were aware of being deprived of the freedom *to* work. Some of them wanted to go on earning as much as they could for as long as they could, and if that is what they wanted they should be able to do so. Others liked their jobs, however contrary it may seem, precisely because their jobs *did* limit their freedom. They were now uncomfortable because they could do what they

* In this distinction, though not in its application to older people, we have followed the usage of Isaiah Berlin in his *Four Essays on Liberty*, pp.118–72, and are grateful to Dr Botros of King's College, London, for drawing it to our attention and for the discussions about it.

wanted to do instead of what they were told to do by an employer who paid them to do what they were told, supported not just by a command of money but by a work ethic which seems incompatible with a notion of freedom that stresses the value of not having to work, and, indeed, by the web of customary attitudes that in the second age has become second nature to that age. Such people had so successfully internalised the imperatives of a society devoted to work that they could not happily choose something different. They would rather go on catching that 8.10 every day without giving a thought to the other things that they might do if, half way to the station, they flung up their hands and decided to miss the train. They would rather be human metronomes. People can shy away from freedom as a horse kept blinkered rears back from the unexpected. So we are not by any means resting our argument on the claim that all people at this stage of life like being free, merely that they can be. Our particular interest in this book is in seeing who, when they have the chance, ventures out and who pulls back.

Those who venture out can be regarded as having positive freedom.

The 'positive' sense of the word 'liberty' derives from the wish on the part of the individual to be his own master. I wish my life and decisions to depend on myself, not on external forces of whatever kind. I wish to be the instrument of my own, not of other men's, acts of will. I wish to be a subject, not an object; to be moved by reasons, by conscious purposes, which are my own, not by causes which affect me, as it were, from outside. I wish to be somebody, not nobody; a doer – deciding, not being decided for, self-directed and not acted upon by external nature or by other men as if I were a thing, or an animal, or a slave incapable of playing a human role, that is, of conceiving goals and policies of my own and realizing them.*

* Berlin, *On Liberty*, pp.131–2. The idea of individuals being their own masters no doubt needs to be qualified, as Plato did. 'Is not "master of oneself" an absurd expression? A man who was master of himself would presumably be also subject to himself, and the subject would be master; for all these terms

In pursuing our enquiry, if we were not too stringent about it
and not too solemn, we hoped we should find some people in
some such state, in the positive form of the third age rather than
its negative form, in some active way not conforming to the
stereotype of the white-haired figure seen through the window,
sitting in soft slippers by the gas-fire, hands crossed, with face
all gentleness and eyes all a friendly twinkle in the occasional
moments when not dozing off; and not like Mr Stanley, one of
our informants, who regarded his new state with distaste, saying
'I can eat when I want'. He had much preferred to eat when he
had to.

The two notions, negative and positive, which we refer to
throughout the book, are the opposites within a whole. The
desire to be free from interference by others is very much the
same as the desire to be your own master. But there is still an
important difference between being free from interference by
other masters and using that freedom to make something lively
out of being your own. Not to be acted upon is one thing; to
act, another. For some people it may be sweet enough just to
breathe in the air of freedom as long as no one else is metering
it. But such freedom is not much use if it freezes people into a
paralysis, unable to act, even though nothing except themselves
is preventing them from acting. Negative freedom is so precious
because it is one of the conditions of autonomy (implying that
a person has the power of self-government and uses it) for
individuals and groups, but it is the autonomy itself which
matters.

Whether or not people succeed in taking advantage of their
opportunity is dependent upon many considerations, money not
the least, and we have tried not to close our minds to any of
them. But the one to which we have given most prominence is

---

apply to the same person . . . I think, however, the phrase means that within
the man himself, in his soul, there is a better part and a worse; and that he is
his own master when the part which is better by nature has the worse under
its control. It is certainly a term of praise; whereas it is considered a disgrace,
when, through bad breeding or bad company, the better part is overwhelmed
by the worse, like a small force outnumbered by a multitude. A man in that
condition is called a slave to himself and intemperate.' *The Republic of Plato*,
ed. F.M. Cornford (Oxford: Clarendon Press, 1941), pp.121–2.

to do with the notion of time-structure which was developed in Michael Young's previous book, *The Metronomic Society*. This touches on what is an outstanding difference between having a paid job and not having one: people with a job are enclosed within a complex scaffolding of time in which many decisions about what has to be done at 8.10, 9, or 10.15, or between 3 and 3.30, or at all, are laid down in a mesh of prescriptive detail which becomes part of them, the habits by which they know themselves and are known by others. The person without a job can still have a scaffolding, indeed needs to have one. Nature is the mistress who lets people alone for much of the time if only her insistent calls for food and sleep at regular intervals are not denied. In between the fixed points when people have to acknowledge their ultimate controller, their time has empty holes in it which have to be filled one by one by making a whole series of choices, and fixing them into a meaningful structure, even if the actual choices which are made seem thin and uninspiring.

If people who move out, or are thrown out, of work, and the structure of time that it creates, fail to make something of their new freedom, they can become diminished rather than enlarged, shrivel up rather than expand. This was famously evident from a well-known study, not of retired but of unemployed people, in the Great Depression. It was made by Marie Jahoda and her colleagues in 1930 in Marienthal, an industrial village thirty-five minutes' train ride from Vienna. For want of orders its sole factory, a textile mill, had been closed down, then pulled down. In Marienthal, it turned out, not only had the work ethic been undermined, the time ethic had gone too, which in most of the societies which human beings have made for themselves is what keeps people busy and safeguarded from the abyss of a structure-less eternity. In this village leisure was no boon but a 'tragic gift'. The men's lives had collapsed. When they were asked what they had done with a day, they could not remember much beyond sleeping and eating, partly because they had eaten very little in a place where they had killed and eaten most of their cats and dogs. They did not bother to keep time. Their wives complained that although their husbands had nothing to do they were never on time for meals. They did not carry watches. 'Of one hundred

23

men eighty-eight were not wearing a watch and only thirty-one of these had a watch at home.'* For the men of Marienthal time was no longer scarce, and that is the one scarcity which people need plenty of. The vision left by that study was a powerful one, very far from that of a grannie in her rocking chair before her TV set. Marienthal was men in cloth caps and worn shoes, shrunken by the cold of winter, hands deep in pockets to keep warm, shuffling aimlessly back and forth down the same stretch of street, like limp lions in a cage of their own making, their eyes down, their spirits down. They did not know what else to do with themselves. They had been overtaken by apathy. In our enquiry we wanted to spot not only those who viewed their new state as a fine freedom but also others, if there were any, who regarded it as the opposite. They might highlight not only the meaning of positive freedom in contemporary circumstances but also of the negative version.

In Marienthal it was men who received the tragic gift and not the women. Unemployment was a grievous blow for them too. But it did not strike at the time-structure of their lives. The lionesses were not as limp as the lions. The women's lives were almost as full as ever, cooking what little there was to cook, caring for children, cleaning their houses, making-do. This is reminder enough, if reminder is needed, that work is still work without being paid and, altogether, that the pattern over the life-cycle of both paid and unpaid work is very different for women. They were represented in our sample and a chapter is devoted specifically to them.

How many are at all like the men or the women of Marienthal? How many are already firmly established in the third age in its positive form? We could not, despite the generosity of the Leverhulme Trust who gave us a grant for the work, conduct a survey drawing on a representative sample for the whole country. Our resources would not stretch to that. But we could track down older people in one particular place, the London Borough of Greenwich being our choice,** invite them to join in the

* M. Jahoda et al, *Marienthal: The Sociography of an Unemployed Community*, p.67.
** See Appendix 2 on the place and a detailed description of the sample.

discussion with us on whatever they wanted to say about the ways in which they were managing when no longer in work, calculating that if we could spot some of the conditions of positive freedom in Greenwich that could spark off some further enquiries on a much larger scale in the future.

Having chosen our district we next had to choose our sample within it. We could have gone for people in their seventies or eighties or people over the statutory pensionable ages of sixty-five for men and sixty for women. That would have produced a more conventional enquiry into the 'old'. But we wanted younger people who would include an important new category of the 'early retired', people who were in transition from ordinary work and having to make the adjustment (or failing to make the adjustment) of moving from the second age of paid employment to the third age as we have begun to describe it. We thought we might learn most from people perhaps unsure whether they still belonged, on the one hand, to the ordinary working population of which they had been part until recently or, on the other hand, to the 'old'. But the clinching consideration was that since we believed there is an increasing readiness for change in the way in which older people regard themselves, and are regarded, our interest was even more in how things might be when people in their fifties and early sixties themselves grow older, than in how things are in the present for those who have already left those years behind. In the book our interest is not only in report; it is in speculating about possibility, in how things might be in the future.* So we decided to confine our sample to men between fifty** and the pensionable age of sixty-five, and women between fifty and sixty, who had for whatever reason left full-time employment within the last two years. In Chapter 2 we are

---

* Milan Kundera in *The Art of the Novel* (London: Faber, 1988), says that this is also the function of the novel, to show what might be – 'A novel examines not reality but existence. And existence is the realm of human possibilities, everything that man can become, everything he's capable of' (p.42).
** The House of Commons Employment Committee in *The Employment Patterns of the Over 50s*, speaking of discrimination on grounds of age, said that 'Fifty, however, is generally accepted as being a watershed in life, and seems to be the age from which difficulties are generally experienced, although they may intensify later' (Vol.1, p.ix).

bringing in two further groups of people who had been employed in a local car factory and a local hospital. We have throughout, in order to protect identities, given assumed names to the people we saw. As we explain in Appendix 2, the main field work was done in 1984 and 1985 with some follow-up interviews being done in later years. Our informants in the main sample were also asked to complete diaries which showed in detail how they used their time.

*　　*　　*

While industrialisation has gradually blurred the boundaries between the old social classes thrown up by the occupational structure, and weakened their hold, it has created two new classes whose members are defined not by their position within an occupational structure but by not having an occupation at all of the ordinary sort; and then, by mixing statecraft with the improvement of health, each of the new classes – the young and the old – has been enlarged. The new leisure classes are as much a product of industrialisation as the old occupational ones. Without the increased productivity which industrialisation has yielded it would not have been possible to support so many people who are not themselves contributing to their own upkeep. They are prevented from doing so.

A singular fact about the new age-classes is that their members have not behaved as though that is what they were. They have not acted together to advance their common interests. Not that we expect the inconsistencies between biological and social ageing, deep-lying though they are, to generate quick new solidarities which will decisively shift the course of social development. But it would be an initial step for older people, whether or not they have a sense of loss when they no longer have paid work, to make something distinctive of the freedom they have gained to control their own time. The question is whether this is happening already. Are people in the third age making use of their new opportunities?

TWO

Life at Work: the Factory and the Hospital

'It's like giving myself little injections of happiness at least once every twenty-four hours.'   *Mr Walters, Thamesmead*

The age-classes we have been describing in the last chapter are distinct enough, the boundaries still marked. When people leave their paid work, even if they do not necessarily enter the third age, at least they are candidates for it. But we do not want to give the impression that they can cut themselves off from their second age in their previous working life as though it had not existed. This is rare. They do not wake up as new-born if elderly infants on their first day of retirement. They are still ex-clerks, ex-machinists, ex-lawyers, ex-nothing-in-particular. Even though the 'ex' part will fade, it will never be extinguished. The point of this chapter is to make quite clear how much of a continuum there is. To find out how their jobs affect people in later life would mean following them through from work into retirement, knowing enough about the work to spot some of its lasting effects. This we could not do with our main sample, who had already left work behind when we saw them, but we could have a closer look at our other two groups of workers, chosen for contrast, and draw on them for illustration. We asked them how they spent their time while they were still in work, even going into some detail about it because if one is going to consider the effect left on people by their work one needs to bear in mind the sort of niches that they have filled in a complex and specialised economy before they become their own masters and mistresses with a freedom to do what they want that they have never had before. What people have done before they attain this freedom will always influence what they do afterwards, and sometimes it will do so decisively. This is what happened in the two groups we chose. The third age had so many attractions for the one group because the second age had so few, and so few attractions for the other because the second age had so many.

A local Ford car factory gave us one group. The plant faced backwards into the past. It employed exclusively men, who had worked almost continuously full-time on manual manufacturing jobs since leaving school at fourteen – a typical pattern in the middle decades of the century. The hospital which gave us the other group pointed more to the future: it was in a service industry, staffed largely by women working part-time after discontinuous employment.

The machining plant, in the Woolwich end of the Borough of Greenwich, was a small one for Ford. It had been under threat of closure for some years, employing only a few hundred people at the time we first visited it, making oil and water pumps, con rods and axle housings. It had served its turn producing fuses before Ford bought it in 1955 from the old Royal Arsenal where munitions had been made. Ford converted it for the manufacture of car and truck components – this in a period of full employment when employers were competing fiercely for labour. The Japanese car industry had hardly been heard of, or, if it had, was derided for its sterile imitativeness.

The main Ford plant at Dagenham, across the river on the north bank of the Thames, drew workers from the south who before the Woolwich factory was opened had to cross over the water every day on an antiquated ferry. The plan behind the Woolwich factory was that if the journey across the water could be cut out many more people could be enticed into Fords, especially from all those who still travelled to work by bus.

In a new era of Japanese competition and labour surplus what had made sense then no longer did. The Woolwich factory was thought too small. Higher management might at any moment decide to reverse their earlier policy of dispersal and close the plant completely. At the time of our study they had not yet reached that but they were offering older men inducements to retire. The men would not necessarily get such generous terms again. An opportunity had come it would be foolhardy not to seize. As soon as it was announced, most of the workers at Woolwich with a chance rushed to put their names down for this 'Special Early Retirement', as the scheme was called. The name also gave them a label, 'early retired', which they would mostly be glad to adopt, even though they would all also register officially as unemployed in order to draw unemployment benefit.

The Woolwich plant had a good industrial relations record, with little of the turbulence that had made the company a byword for conflict.* The plant had many older employees. They had been a stable workforce. Their length of service made them unlike many of the people in our general sample who had switched from one job to another and into and out of employment and unemployment. Small as the plant was, it had recently staged the largest long-service dinner – for those with more than twenty-five years' service – in the recent history of Ford of Britain. The industrial relations manager and the union convener knew and respected each other; they had an established working relationship which nevertheless stopped well short of cosiness. The union was committed to opposing redundancies, but Special Early Retirement was not redundancy. In discussions with us the manager occasionally referred to voluntary redundancies, at which point the convener would wince at the word and remind him of the correct name.

The class background

We interviewed the forty people who had applied for early retirement before it was known which of them would get it, and the following year we saw again the nineteen of them who had been successful and had now left. One and all, they were eager to leave for other reasons besides the generous terms. Their jobs had been hard. They belonged to a traditional, tough, male working class. The toughest of the tough were promoted up the ladder to managerial jobs in a 'working-class company', and some of them became legendary, like 'Frosty', the Ford executive

* See H. Beynon, *Working for Ford* (London: Allen Lane, 1973).

from the 1950s who was still spoken of in the 1980s with respect and even affection, as much for his harshness as despite it. He sounded like an industrial Duke of Wellington. The physical work was hard, often gruelling, in a kind of metal-bashing manufacture which is now fast disappearing. They had little to look back on as fondly as they did on Frosty. Born in a pre-meritocratic age before the 1944 educational reforms, they were the children of manual workers who became manual workers as a matter of course, and in some ways had even worse life-chances than their parents. They were caught up in the Hitler war. This stopped them from getting or competing for apprenticeships in the skilled trades which were then the common goal of working-class boys with any ambition.

Larry Carroll, for example, was three-quarters of the way towards becoming a skilled setter-turner on a lathe when German planes, in burying the factory where he worked, buried his chances too. Many others were called up because, being unskilled, they were not in a reserved occupation considered essential in a war-time economy. They returned after the war with experience no longer of value this side of the Normandy Beaches but with a pressing need for a well-paid job. Get one and they could start a family.

In talking to us they seemed to take a strangely foreshortened view of their lives. They had not been employed so much for forty years as for eighty thousand hours, always paid by the hour or, at best, the day. They had never been sure in any particular job whether their next hour would not be their last in it and, as they recalled it, it was as though their youth in the 1940s was hardly more than an hour away. As manual workers they reached their maximum hourly wage in real terms in their early twenties when they became entitled to an adult wage, and there they stuck, rising only when other workers of the same kind did so too.

If they could now choose a way of life for themselves it would not be so much a second chance as the first. They knew, with varying degrees of bitterness or with none, that they had been locked into their kind of work and life by the conditions into which they had been born. They had never expected work to be enjoyable, and it had not been. It was something more or less unpleasant which had to be done for the sake of the money.

The workplace

The place was dirty. To avoid getting wet feet from the pools of coolant which leaked from the machines took as much local topographical knowledge as if it were a marsh. The second disadvantage was the noise. The hum and buzz of the machines was so loud that when standing near them communication had to be in a sign language which newcomers had to learn. The third disadvantage was the strenuousness of the work, especially for those who despite the cranes and conveyors still had to carry heavy weights or hammer forcefully away at a piece of metal to get it into shape. The fourth was that whatever they did was for the purposes of payment minutely timed by a management which could almost have been called the time and moneygement. People sold their minutes even if they were paid by the hour. The fifth and most severe disadvantage – the monotony – resulted from the short cycles or routines into which they were tied after being timed. These had little to do with nature and a lot to do with the requirements of the work-cycles of the individual machines and of the overall machine-like organisation. It was not difficult to understand why the men should be glad to leave the second age behind.

The factory was given a series of monthly quotas by head office for so many axles and pumps of different sorts and the quotas were converted into a series of timed tasks for every minute for every man on every line. Line referred less to a row of machines than to a line as a metaphor, to convey the idea that the machines and the men attached to them were organised in sequences, as if they were in a straight line, when in fact they were often enough in a wiggly one, winding through the mechanical marsh on the factory floor. Thus a target output of so many axles a day could become twenty for each standard hour in an eight-hour day. On a line responsible for a particular process the endlessly-repeated cycle of the men on it could be down to a few minutes. The machines did not synchronise with each other perfectly as we were told they did to a much greater extent in Japan. There a company not only made cars but made the machines to make cars. In Woolwich the lack of fit between the machines gave some tiny latitude to their operators. But it was still true that a man had to repeat himself every few seconds or minutes throughout the day, every day, in order to fulfil his quota. The monotony, far from getting more bearable, could get worse with the years, and the prospective relief relief indeed.

The measurements did not stop at minutes. The factory hand-book recorded these timings to three decimal places. Drill-ream-ing a spot-face was to take 2.059 minutes, drilling cotter-pins 1.729 and so forth. The whole process to which these were applied was made up of five units and the total allowed for the particular process was also given with the same notional pre-cision: 9.549 minutes. It was, of course, recognised that devi-ation from the norms would be common; but these forbiddingly exact times were still formally used as the basis for calculating productivity and efficiency. The precision was paralleled in the slip which recorded the benefits to which the early leavers were entitled. This counted the service given up to the man's fortieth birthday and then afterwards, separately, on a higher tariff. Both were added up in years, months and days made up of so many minutes to give a figure in thousands of pounds but exact to the last penny.

The time-study book could not allow for machines breaking down. When they did there was a welcome pause. Len Watts had a senile machine. He was a quiet, polite man who considered each of our questions carefully before he answered, as though each question was a block of hot metal that could be dangerous unless handled with the utmost caution. Called a welder, he was also a kind of blacksmith. When he first began work in the factory his welding machine was as new to the job as he was himself. During its first years the welds were perfect. But when the machine lost its youthful perfection Len became more and more fond of it. Since the two pieces of metal which form a front axle had fallen out of alignment Len had to become the adjuster, which meant he had to hit the metal with a heavy hammer. After nineteen years, as the machine had become less perfect he had become more so, knowing just how hard to hit according to the extent to which the two pieces were out of kilter. The straightening took him about twenty seconds. The exercise of that little bit of skill and muscle made the job slightly less boring. On the day we interviewed him he was thinking more of beer than of axles. On the previous night he had been with his son, a tree surgeon with an enviably varied job in the open air, to the Charles Dickens pub in St Katharine's Dock on the other side of the Thames. It was sunny and they had a long and pleasant talk, drinking their beer by the river.

Len was counted as a 'direct' worker because he worked on the line producing finished components. In addition there were many 'indirects' who supported the 'directs', their timing being often derivative without being any the less demanding. Mr King was a lavatory cleaner. The most urgent thing he had to do in his day was to make sure that every lavatory had paper in it in the early morning. He was tied in to other men's digestive cycles.

The many inspectors of quality did not themselves produce the parts; they inspected what others had produced. George Parker was a buy-off inspector in the Quality Control Department. He checked the pumps – their tap holes, bores, gear chambers, porosity – as they came off the line at a rate of a hundred and fifty per hour. In his observations he invariably followed exactly the same sequence on each pump because it enabled him to spot any faults the more surely and the more immediately. A few years ago George had had a heart-attack; since then he had lost interest in the job and was 'beginning to get bored' – after twenty-nine years.

The security guards worked almost as repetitively, at least on nights. They had to make fast patrols around the whole plant, punching fifteen clocks around the factory to prove they had been there at precisely the scheduled time. This had to be done if the company was to get all the reductions it could on its fire and burglary insurance. Including indirects with directs, the whole factory, although stacked with individual machines, was itself like a single large and highly articulated one. Insofar as it is a kind of machine, such a factory will no doubt eventually be replaced by robots. Robots have so far only taken over some of the processes.

If the repetitiveness was as tedious as it seemed to us, why was there not more complaint? It was as if most of the men had been doing jobs like these for so long that this was their only idea of work. They had become habituated not just to the particular job on which they were engaged currently but, over a lifetime, to jobs like it. Self-selection was in play as well as habit. People who could not put up with the repetitiveness either never came to Fords or left soon after, while people who liked it or had a marked tolerance, or in extreme cases an obsession, for it were the ones who came, stayed and did what was expected of them. A man like Mr Paine who prided himself on only having been three minutes late in thirty years could be relied on to keep a very steady pace.

Peter Semple thought he had learned his time-sense from his early experience in the Royal Arsenal: 'They paid the best penny around here. It was piecework. So when I came here I was already primed up; you can't do piecework here but you can save time.' He positively relished working fast, the same one day as another. The urge spilled over into his home, and would into his life after work. Watching his wife move round the space in his kitchen, he wanted to rationalise what she did. She eventually divorced him. Mr Quarry said his wife also complained that he put a stop-watch on her. The effects could spill over in other ways as well. Simon Davis remarked on his irritation with supermarkets:

> In Fords what counts is to get the pieces down the line. When an old lady puts her basket down in the wrong place and people can't get by I get terribly irritated. It's worse when someone talks to the girl at the checkout about Mrs Brown's baby. When they dither I get annoyed. I think that's all my Ford training.

If the major disadvantage of the work was the monotony imposed by the machinery, the disadvantage was at least softened by the faint pulsing of more natural rhythms. When there was sun outside it peeped in through the fanlights which ran right down the factory's saw-tooth roofs. The sun cut down the electricity bill. The working day also retained some strange rhythms of its own. A kind of wave motion ran through the day's production, beginning slowly at the start of a shift while the men on later machines in a series waited (as if for a tide) for the first of that day's output to reach them. The hourly rate accelerated after that and reached a peak in the late morning. In the afternoon there was a gradual slackening till knocking-off time. These ups and downs over the course of the day were clearly shown by the fluctuations in the electricity load curve for the factory.

The management did not like what they thought of as the disorderliness of it. They wanted the same steady output in each and every hour; this was (we were told) the habit of more sensible, more disciplined workers in Ford's German factories. The English preferred to vary the pace. This way they could accumulate a reserve in the morning while they were at their freshest – they talked about 'winning' time in the morning – so that if things went wrong in the afternoon they could still achieve their daily quota. They could reduce the monotony of going at the same pace throughout the day by themselves exercising some control over the timing. So there *was* a daily rhythm, and also a seasonal one. August was the occasion for the annual holiday shutdown when only the maintenance men and toolmakers stayed on to repair old machines and install new ones. After the seasonal return to work, with Christmas to look forward to and save up for, production increased – went with a swing, as it was put – until the end of the year, only to fall off thereafter.

Other complaints

The worst fate was having nothing to do. Eric Tanner was a skilled toolmaker in the maintenance department. As a skilled man he was free from the pressures of the line but not from those of the plant. One day began, like others, at 7.15, with him standing at his bench waiting but with nothing at all to do. His first wait was usually at least half an hour. Then the foreman might give him a ticket for a job replacing the bushes that guide drills into the con rods. This took him an hour and a half. Then again, for perhaps three hours, nothing. His two mates chatted.

He wrote out chords, familiarising himself with passages which had not gone with complete smoothness in his piano practice the night before. Then, say, at one o'clock there was a breakdown on an oil-pump unit. Suddenly it was all go. It took a hectic hour to repair, after which there was another lull. The younger fitters continued to make up their own sets of tools, but Eric's set had been complete long ago. Tools last. No need to replace them frequently. He still has the micrometer he first got when he was fifteen.

> This is the job that people want, getting paid for doing nothing. But not me. If we'd been busy it wouldn't have been so bad, but I stood there for three years with my hands behind my back. My brain was going. Even if I didn't have a penny I wouldn't go back there now. No way. I'm starting to live a little since I left.

An even more general complaint was about the large amount of overtime and, more emphatically still, about the shiftwork which forced people to try to override their internal body-rhythms.* For many years the pattern was to work 'weeks about', that is one week on days, the next week on nights, maximising both the utilisation of the machines and the wear on their attendants. This is known to be one of the most taxing of shift patterns. Seven days on nights is long enough for the biological rhythms of most people to get sufficiently accustomed to the new dispensation for them to be able to sleep fairly happily by day and eat fairly happily by night. But just when an internal adjustment is being made it is back again to days and a reversal of what the body has begun to learn in the previous week.

No one had a good word for nightwork, apart from the extra pay. George Parker said, 'The first night, Monday, you'd go in and you'd be fighting to keep your eyes open.' Bill Darling couldn't get used to the effect on his appetite.

---

* The human cost of nightwork is only now beginning to be properly assessed in the light of such facts as that the nuclear accident at Three Mile Island began at 4 a.m., the one at Chernobyl at 1.30 a.m. and the explosion at Union Carbide in Bhopal, India, at 12.40 a.m.

Week about isn't good. Eating was the worst thing. I'd get out of bed in the evening and the wife would cook me a dinner and I couldn't eat it. She'd say, 'I don't know why you won't eat it', and I'd say, 'Well, when I get home in the morning I'll cook you a dinner and see if you feel like eating it'. I did thirty years of week about and still didn't get used to it.

Greg Reid may have been exaggerating but he was only voicing what many men thought when he said that the shiftwork and the overtime were, literally, killers. According to Greg, people were apt to die quite young from illnesses brought on by shift-work, or from suicides precipitated by the consequential in-fidelities. 'Whilst they were working other things were going on at home.'

Not only the monotony but the general strain of the work, whether on nights or days, became more trying as people got older. Like other manual workers whose jobs draw heavily on their physical strength, they noticed their failing powers. Physical ageing mattered much more than in non-manual occupations where it may actually be an advantage (up to a point) to be older. The older workers could not keep up with the pace in the same way as younger ones. 'After the age of fifty', said Mr Grey, 'the pace gets more wearing. You can't move around like a youngster can.'

Older men could not avoid noticing that they were, as John Livermore said, 'tiring more easily and reasoning more slowly'. Nor could they carry weights as readily as they once had. Despite the conveyors and other aids, there were still plenty of jobs which required human muscle. Len Watts not only had to use his hammer but had to keep lifting axles which weighed fifty-six pounds each, although there was an overhead transporter which was supposed to do it. It was as much of an effort to use it as to lift by hand, and it took longer, but the lifting tired him more than it used to. Another man with a weak chest had been told by his doctor that he should not lift anything with outstretched arms; but he kept to himself what his doctor had said. He feared he would otherwise be put on to lighter and more boring work. Some people also concealed their age from everyone on the shop floor so that they would not be given more demeaning jobs.

Others whose emphysema, for example, was made worse by the vapour of the coolant, whose deafness was increased by the noise or whose ulcers were aggravated by the nightwork, were only too glad of a switch to lighter work, as were some of those who, without particular disabilities, were just feeling their age. They hoped to be put on to less demanding machines, less demanding lines or on to indirect jobs which were less fatiguing even if they were also more boring. Such people were liable to shorten their subjective expectation of life, with the old retirement age of sixty-five being a prospective cut-off point beyond which, if they survived at all, they did not expect themselves to be good for much. Sixty-two-year-old Mr Davis, a former footballer, ruefully said that 'Many of my friends are like me in getting close to the cemetery.' For such people early retirement had a special attraction. 'I want', said Bill Darling, 'to get time for myself before it's too late.' Many of them had noticed that ex-workers who returned to visit the factory looked so much better than they used to look. The pallor had gone from their skin.

The draw of the wages

But for all the hardship, the factory offered one great boon which was carried over into retirement: the wages, especially for semi-skilled and unskilled men. Bill Darling remembered responding to his young wife's dislike of nightwork by agreeing, finally, to look for work without it. Ford was paying three and tuppence an hour at the time. Like other men, he remembered precisely what his hourly rate had been at different periods of his life, back over thirty or forty years. He applied to a firm that made batteries for use at night, and made them only by day.

> The manager there said 'How much do you want?'. I thought, I won't be hard on him, so I said, 'Well three shillings, two and eleven'. 'You believe in starting at the top and working down', he said, 'You'll be lucky to get

one and eleven, one and ten.' So that was the difference in
those days.

Bill and his wife decided to put up with the nightwork. Now
that he was retiring, he was on the whole glad he had done so,
not because he liked the shiftwork but because of the money it
yielded.

Eric Tanner did not have much good to say about his working
life except the money. 'Lovely the fifties were. I bought the
Anglia just like that – £550, no trouble. We had the two boys,
a new car and we were buying this house. As soon as you said
"Fords" you got the loan.' The wages they had earned in the
past supported their standard of life in the present. Ray Flower
spread his arms out wide in his comfortably furnished living
room.

> I mean this is Fords. Fords bought this. Twenty years ago I
> had no money, no house. I don't regret leaving Fords and
> I don't regret going to Fords. When I went to Fords the
> first week's wages were £18 compared with £8 at the
> Arsenal. When I came home I threw it all up in the air and
> said to my wife, 'Look, look, we're going to be millionaires'.

In the past the hourly rate was almost all that mattered.
This had changed. Fringe benefits had become gradually more
important and had come to figure ever larger in collective bar-
gaining – the Ford cars that employees had the right to buy at
preferential prices, the holidays and, above all, the pensions.
When there was full employment Eric Tanner, like many others,
was accustomed to move from one job to another. He only had
to hear on the grapevine about a job with marginally better
hourly rates to ask for his cards and be off. If he left one day
he could have a dozen jobs on the next. But, unlike Fords, the
small firms offered no pensions, so as Eric got older and had
less future left he became correspondingly more fearful about it.
He settled into Fords.

On top of their weekly occupational pension they could, after
leaving, draw unemployment benefit for one year, subject to the
rather nominal condition that they remained eligible for work.

One of our informants was, to his horror, sent for a job with another engineering firm in Lewisham. But all was well: he managed to convince them he was too old. No Puritan Ethic for him, not at his age.

They also received lump sums. These ranged from £12,000 to £18,000 depending on the length of service and whether or not the service had been uninterrupted – Eric Tanner was penalised for having left the firm in search of better wages before he returned to it. The special terms added around £4,000 to the lump sum entitlements of those who had served upwards of thirty years. These sums were crucial in tiding them over the awkward – potentially disastrous – gap between leaving the company and being entitled to the State pension. Some of them made careful financial projections before they accepted the offer, calculating the extent to which they would be able to substitute expenditure from capital for income over the next few years. Others had not been given enough information to do this, and relied initially on the prevailing opinion that the amounts, being unusually high, were not on any account to be missed.

Most of the men also owned their houses rent- and interest-free. This gave them not only a sound capital base but the opportunity, if they wished, to realise some of the market value of a house which, however modest, was in London and move to somewhere cheaper. They had paid for it. The obligations of mortgage and family were precisely what had kept them in line at Fords. For two out of three of the men their asset now made it easier to leave.

Several spoke of having 'served their time'. They were not referring to the apprenticeship, which many had missed, but to their work in the factory as a kind of punishment which entitled them to what was to come, as if they had served a sentence in a prison from which they were now being released. One man said that work at Fords was so hard that every year was the equal of two elsewhere so he had 'done' eighty years in all. Eric Tanner was not the only one hoping to be able 'to live a little'.

The gates close

At departure there were therefore no regrets. After a long spell in such a factory one might have expected some solemnity. Not them: they did not anticipate (or get) any recognition from a hard-boiled management not notable for its benevolence. They had learned to understand what it was like, from Frosty onwards, and they did not expect any thanks. They knew they would have to work up to 4 p.m. on the last day. Come the last trump and it was a quick glass of sherry with the new plant manager who was having a short spell at Woolwich on his way up to a larger domain. The sherry, for beer-drinkers, was the only little gesture of a ritualistic nature.

This new manager could not reminisce about the days when the plant, before the redundancies began to bite, had been far more of a little society, with regular dances, dinners and outings to express its solidarity. It was just a sherry and a hand-shake. No tears. Keith Quarry said of the gatekeeper:

> I think I upset Joe Turner. When we went through the gate for the last time I said 'Well, I never had any close friend-ships there. I just went there to work and that was it.' 'Thanks very much', he said, 'we've been working with you for all these years.'

For Greg Reid the last day was much like any other Friday, without any special feeling about it.

> The last day, well, I was packing things up, making sure I didn't owe the Ford Motor Company anything, clothes, -tools and so on. When I got home I took the old attaché case that I'd had for years to take my things in to the works and threw it away. It just came to me as the natural thing to do.

Bob Church was much the same. 'I never noticed it, going through the gates. It's something you think about before, going through the gates for the last time, but we all went through together and I hardly noticed it.'

But the factory remained a presence all the same. Men's bodies bore the imprint. George Parker, whom we have already quoted, had not only found the shiftwork particularly trying. For thirty years he had not got used to it, and now, months after leaving, the reverse curse was that he could not get used to being without it.

> Since I packed up do you know the weeks I'm supposed to be doing nightwork I can't sleep. It's unbelievable. Even now I keep dozing off throughout the day every other week. It's queer the habits you get, even going to the toilet.

Most men also showed they still belonged to the other side of the gates by substituting one set of routines for another. Bob Church had fitted himself up with a very marked routine when we saw him for the first time at home. He had planned the redecoration and refitting of his house as meticulously as if he were planning a new line of drilling machines. He was a Yorkshireman by origin and was (he would put in a 'therefore') keen on cricket. The day before the interview there had been a one-day Test Match. In a way he would have liked to have sat down in front of the TV and watched the cricket all day. But this was a luxury he did not feel he could afford. He had to 'work' the whole day, in one respect as though he were still in the factory, in another respect not, for while he was still employed he could only find snatches of time for important tasks like painting. He didn't give up at all until half past five when the highlights of the game were shown.

He couldn't do any serious work on the following day, a Wednesday, because since his 'retirement' he had taken to play-ing not cricket but bowls for the whole of every Wednesday afternoon and, as he could not let himself and his friends down, it was not worth starting on the kitchen at all if he only had a morning for it. On Thursday he would make a good early start and turn off the water at the mains at 7 a.m. sharp. It would make his son get up early to fill the bath, the kettle and a few jugs. Most of the other men were handymen like Bob, delighted to exercise their skill – when 'you're your own supervisor' – in improving their own personal investment. They were treasuring the planned work that remained to be done on their own holding before embarking on another round of improvements.

Keith Quarry was unusual: both a Council tenant and something of an entrepreneur. He would not buy his house because he disapproved on political grounds of selling Council houses. But he made up for not having his own property by cultivating a little job, helping his son with his software consultancy business, taking computer disks to a mainframe computer in central London where the analysis was done, and chasing up the slow payers. He relished the personal contacts the business brought him, as he did his visits to his grandson's public school. His kitchen was studded with photographs of this grandson smiling out from the ranks of different sporting teams against a backdrop of parklands and large Victorian Gothic buildings. He liked to talk to the headmaster about his grandson's prospects, which did not include working in an axle factory for the car industry.

Eric Tanner had a vocation. We have already seen him writing down chords in the toolroom. He was brought up in poverty. He could recall his mother's fine singing voice in the one room which was all the family had. Music was in his blood but he had had no chance to study it. He had to go out to work early to earn money for his family. Not until he was twenty-two was he able to buy a piano. Ever since then, for nearly forty years, his dream had been to become a pianist, full-time. It had not helped him to have passed on his enthusiasm to one of his sons who was now the principal clarinettist in a national orchestra. This son had used their front room to teach pupils so as to pay his way through college and this meant Eric could not use the room as well until his son was qualified. He did not regret that. But he did regret that his other son was in engineering and that music was of so little interest to anyone else at Woolwich. He had seen to it that his musical son's achievements had been featured more than once in *Ford News* but no one had commented on it.

There are enough people making cars but there aren't enough making music. When I was standing around doing nothing I was always thinking that I could be at home teaching people, bringing them pleasure and using my time properly.

He was now making up for it, practising several hours a day with enough pupils, mostly children, to make him into a teacher for a few nights a week. If he could get some day-time pupils as well, his cup would be full. Music, and to a lesser extent poetry, was his life, and he could talk endlessly about both. The piano took up most of the living-room and he gestured to it repeatedly, as though to a close friend. His wife observed, wistfully, that it would be nice if they could go out for a drink occasionally. Eric dismissed the idea. His only regret was how little time he had left before age took its toll and his fingers lost their suppleness. He measured out the time left to him. The tempo was hard to keep up with.

The only thing that absolutely stuns me is the galloping of time. I mean, it's Thursday again, isn't it? I don't know what's best, whether it's to stand around for those years and make your life long or (to a gale of laughter) to work hard as I'm doing now and get it all over quickly. I forget which day of the week it is. That doesn't worry me, provided I remember to sign on.

Arnold Carter, a supervisor, did not have such a new occupation. The months after his own shut-down at Woolwich were in some ways more like a holiday. He did not consider himself old enough to retire.

I just tidied up and came home. They asked me if I wanted to go on a retirement course but I said no, I didn't want to go because I didn't consider that I was retiring. If I'd turned round and said I was retiring I'd feel older than I am. I said I was 'leaving'. I've had the offer of a job since then. Although I'm taking early retirement I wouldn't say I'll never work again.

But it did not seem likely that he would. His wife suffered from multiple sclerosis. She came home from a spell in hospital six months before he finished work. She needed constant attention. Fortunately she could still accompany him to vintage car and bike rallies. Inside his garage Arnold had a 1930 Lagonda, a nineteenth-century cross-frame push bike and a 1915 Trident on which he had achieved one of his ambitions by completing the London to Brighton run. Time now 'flashes by, especially the five days between weekends'.

Jack Walters, an Irishman, demonstrated his new independence in yet another way.

On the first day I floated across on Cloud Nine. I thought I knew how I would feel because I hated the bloody place and everything appertaining to it, but I didn't: it started off great and it's got steadily better. Fords stood me in good stead because I was bringing up three children but when that was done and they were on their own feet it just went on and on. I didn't get used to Fords, I just found myself getting involved in hostilities. As the reason for being there lessened, my antipathy heightened.

He enjoyed listening to music, making tapes of records he borrowed from the library, doing a bit of gardening and his new share of the domestic work. His wife had a part-time job, so Jack cleaned the house, did the shopping and simpler ironing, had a cold lunch ready for her. He walked a lot, to the shops or to visit his grandchildren, but in spite of this had put on seven pounds. He called it his contentment fat. His only worry was that he was enjoying retirement too much. He said:

I feel very retired at the moment. I keep telling everyone else – and trying to tell myself – that I'm not retiring really. I'm getting the money and running. But since I've retired I must admit I like the idea. People say 'Don't you ever get bored?' and I say 'No', and I stop and think 'You're not going in on nights this week – yippee!' It's like giving myself little injections of happiness at least once every twenty-four hours.

And he jabbed an imaginary needle into his still muscular forearm.

> Happiness in retirement: it all depends what you've retired from. If I'd had job satisfaction there'd probably be regrets now. But it wasn't like that. I accepted it and I adjusted to it, but that doesn't make me turn round and say, 'Oh, those were the good old days'.

He also illustrated the extent to which a personal history can come into play, rolling up behind a man and staying with him as he ages. Jack's father had been a 'bit of a brute', and Jack had been the last of all his siblings to get away from him. Ever since he had lacked confidence, trying out employment in several fields, all of them military or in some way institutional: the Navy, the police and the RAF. Fords had provided security at the financial level and something against which to rail; it was only now that Jack was coming to realise how much his behaviour was still determined by childhood antagonisms, fears and frustrations.

Despite his happiness Jack later found part-time employment, once again of a uniformed and institutional kind, as a Yeoman of the Painted Hall in the Royal Naval College. He was delighted.

> My job is to look after the public, and on formal occasions to march VIPs up and down to the banqueting hall. I'm dressed up in the full regalia, uniform, hat and so on. I've got job satisfaction for the first time in my life.

The hours suited him well; no rush in the morning, and no interruption to the evening's television. 'For the first time I wake up and look forward to work. My only occasional regret is that I haven't been doing this for longer.' But he gave Fords a little of the credit. 'I got the job because they wanted stability and commitment, and my twenty-nine years at Fords spoke for that.'

His particular history mattered as much for George Parker. At the age of five, after his father had been killed in an accident, he was taken first to what they called the workhouse in Plumstead, now St Nicholas Hospital. 'I stayed there overnight, with all those old men and I was only a little boy.' He was taken on to the orphanage the next day by his mother. They gave him a number and ten minutes later knocked him across the room for forgetting it. He never saw his mother again; she died whilst he was there, but he was only told when he left years later, having been made to write every month for year after year to a dead person.

It was one of those self-supporting places. You was taught to look after yourself. It was hard in there, it was like being in prison actually. It was a Catholic orphanage, they used to dress like priests, though they weren't, and they used to term themselves Brother John and so on. If I had children and I knew they were going in there I'd put them to sleep. It was cruel.

He added, 'I've always thought I'd get on all right; some people can't look after themselves at all. I've been brought up the hard way and it's worked out well for me. They had no need to knock me about but that was their way of doing it.'

On the surface George had little structure to his life. He was divorced and lived on his own. Friday was the day for washing and clearing up the house. On Saturdays his daughter-in-law came with her children. They went down to the club in the evening, and on Sundays he went to his daughter. Otherwise there were no fixed points. 'I lose all track of days. I have to keep marking them off on the calendar if I need to remember something. That doesn't worry me, it's great. Touch wood, I'm never bored.'

When they left the factory our informants also left their work-friends, very few of them keeping up with anyone they had known there, even if they had worked alongside them for thirty years. The solidarity of the workplace had been intense. The men were on the same level, mostly not in competition with each other, but under continuous pressure from management to raise productivity. As they saw it, their work was already hard enough and, in combating the relentless pressure, they were relentless too in their way and as loyal to each other as they could be. No one would overtly take the side of the management for fear of being labelled a 'gaffer's man'.

It turned out to have been a solidarity which attached more to the situation than to the people, vanishing when the factory vanished. Arnold Carter articulated what many of the men hinted at when he referred to his Service days:

> I can remember when I went out of the Air Force. A few months later I bumped into a friend as I was going into a cinema. We'd been very close. But all we had to speak about was 'Have you seen old so-and-so', and after two or three minutes we'd finished the conversation. I walked into the cinema and thought, 'Good Lord, I lived with that bloke for two and a half years'.

It was as if the factory was a shell with a particular resonance as long as you held it to your ear; drop it and communication would be distorted and unsatisfactory. By comparison, casual encounters in the shopping centre were insipid.

Goldthorpe and colleagues in their famous study of another lot of affluent workers, in Luton, compared people whose lives had become 'privatised' with those who had not.* What we saw were workers who withdrew into their homes and families only after they left. The ones who had not were unusual. David Williams, for instance. He had gone back to the plant on a social visit, shaking hands with 'the lads'. According to his wife, he still looked wistfully across at the plant when passing it and mused aloud about what the lads were doing. He also spent a large part of the day in front of the huge television that dominated his living-room as much as Eric's piano dominated his.

Most of the men were in between Eric Tanner and David Williams. Eric, and the others like him, had adopted a new style of life, although based on old interests. For him the gates were starting gates. But others found it more difficult to change their habits. They had got thoroughly used to early rising and did not see any reason to change that just because there was nothing to

* J. Goldthorpe, et al, *The Affluent Worker in the Class Struggle*, p.96.

rise for. Nor did they stay up later (unless they were exceptionally drawn by the late-night film) even though they no longer needed to fear the rigours of the following day. They sometimes felt themselves adrift from the people around them. At weekends they could be uncomfortably aware that their neighbours in the same street were locked into the mini-rituals which had once been so meaningful to them and now were so no longer. Sundays could be sad because there was no Monday to follow, even if Monday had meant returning to a worn-out leg welder in the clatter-clutter of a dirty machine shop.

The hospital

The hospital could scarcely be a greater contrast. The Maternity Hospital had roots in *local* history, well before the National Health Service, going back to its origin as an eight-bed maternity home which had been opened in 1905. Some residents still referred to it as 'Oak Street', after its first location. The redbrick building was set firmly within the community and after its closure its later neglect, vandalisation and eventually destruction (for that is what happened) was the cause of acute distress. Mrs Broad felt it particularly sharply: she lived two streets away and could literally hear the place being knocked down. Whereas the Ford plant was cut off from local housing and shops by a main road, so nearly invisible that when passing in a bus even David Williams could almost forget it was there, the hospital was the opposite.

The Ford components were almost the ultimate in impersonality: interchangeable parts which had to be transported elsewhere to roll off yet another line as part of a car or truck. The hospital was different: however routinised the work of some of its employees, such as Mrs Fisher's continuous sorting of dirty laundry in her basement room, its 'products' were individual human beings. The Ford plant itself was a tiny dependency in a mighty worldwide empire. The hospital was, it is true, part of the National Health Service, the largest employer in Europe, and its closure was only possible because its work could supposedly be done by another hospital within the same system. But it had always had a highly individual character inherited from its past as a voluntary organisation. This was made much of by the Management Committee in 1948 when it published a little history.

> It is said that the day of the voluntary hospital is past, and it is possible that the history of the foundation of the hospital may come to be looked upon as an historical curiosity. Yet those who have had the experience of working at Woolwich may be excused if they are apprehensive lest, in the plan of things to come, the spirit of service which has gained for British nursing its international renown may not receive due recognition.

In early 1984 the hospital nursing and auxiliary staff numbered about 150, most of them women, nearly 60% part-timers. Many of the younger staff and all the nurses were given jobs elsewhere in the NHS after the closure. Others moved off to find work for themselves. The eighteen we interviewed were older workers not medically trained who did not take up further employment, in or out of the NHS. Some of them had been employed at the hospital only a short time, whilst others had seen many generations of pregnant mothers come through the swing-doors one and go out two.

Of the eighteen none had been thinking of retirement before the blow fell. They had become attached to the job even if they had drifted casually into it without the material purposefulness of the Ford workers. One of the informants had had no intention of taking a job there at all but had gone along with a friend who did want one but was nervous about the interview. Both ended up with a job. Mrs Powell also got hers through a friend.

> I went there for a month, temporary, and then I got stuck there. Where I live the woman next door was on the switchboard. I didn't go on the switchboard at first. I was up in the rooms. I went there because they had someone out sick.

She stayed on for thirty-three years as a telephonist, working six or even seven days a week, and she would have been happy to stay a good deal longer.

For her and for most of the others there was no official retirement age. Two of the women were in their seventies, and seven were over sixty. They had seen many women continue working at the hospital into their late seventies. 'When I came there was two ladies in their eighties in the sewing-room. So there must have been something about it to make them stay.' As part-timers they had no anticipation of, and certainly no wish for, a fixed finishing age. This suited the management; they had a stable workforce with hardly any turnover.

They had been so attached that they found it difficult to leave. 'I would', said Mrs Old, 'go back there tomorrow if I could – so would a lot of people. I'd've stayed there till I was pushed out. I had no intentions of leaving.' Since they had expected to carry on working there almost as long as they wished, the shock of the closure was all the greater.

They had not only lost their jobs, they had lost their hospital.

It was like losing a good friend really. Because you tell your children about it, they tell *their* children. It goes all through the family. And why it closed up, I don't know. I mean, people don't stop having babies, do they?

Their identity was bound up in the place.

I must say that when I got your letter then I was quite interested because I was absolutely lost then. There was no hope of my getting a job because nobody would give me those hours and I wasn't prepared to go working full-time again obviously. But now I've been listening all this summer; there was a guard over there for ten months, say, from July until April. And then all this summer you'd stand here, and hear all the glass shattering. Bang, crash, crash, crash! It was absolutely sickening when you think of that beautiful place.

Typically for this kind of work done largely by women, the pay was very low, though it did provide some of them with a sense of independence. One said it gave her her own money – it turned out that she had used it to pay for installing central heating without having to touch the money her husband was bringing home. Although no one was obliged to continue for the sake of the money, no one wanted to leave. People felt they were members of two families, a work family and a home family.

For me it was my home, wasn't it? I loved going over there in winter. Even if it was freezing outside when you opened the door it wasn't the heat, it was something like a mother putting her arms around you and saying 'you're home now'. I know when I was at one hospital function – when I got home the door was locked because my husband had gone to work and the kids had gone to bed. Anyway, I thought to myself 'Oh well, there'll be a bed for me over at the hospital if the kids don't answer the door.' But if the dining-room wanted change – you know – if they run out of change, I was sort of always *there*, you know. 'Would you fetch me some change over?' I was always in and out, even when I wasn't working. Even when I was on holiday once, Mrs West rang. She said, 'What are you doing?'. Got so used to you being there it didn't feel right if you was on holiday.

This happened even at the expense of the ordinary family.

I liked working Sundays – there's something different about Sundays, isn't there? I used to love to get home about 9 o'clock, make myself a pot of tea and make myself comfortable. It was nice. Bank Holidays – we always worked Bank Holidays. Apart from the money there was a holiday atmosphere. Christmas Day! Well, I was in every Christmas Day that I worked there. I used to love it – *loved* Christmas Day there! My children used to say 'Oh Mum, can't you have Christmas morning off?' But I'd say, 'No, no. I'd rather go in.' No – I loved it.

At Christmas a real child was placed in the nativity tableau set up in the hospital chapel. One of the men who had no children himself was as much attached to the hospital as any of the women; this was almost too much for his wife. She 'used to get a bit fed up with it. He didn't always have to go in at Christmas, but he *wanted* to go. He thought other men have got children and we've got no children so he used to go in and he liked it.'

The working hours went some way towards explaining the attachment.

> Just mornings – I did six hours in the mornings, Monday to Friday – weekends off. It fitted in lovely with the family because of having the weekends off. That was nice hours. I think it was *that* that first attracted me to it. I used to think it was lovely being home every Saturday and Sunday – I was pleased to think I was not neglecting them. I was pleased to think my hours was so regular – I knew to always work my day out like, I never had any split duties, or nights or nothing. Lovely hours, lovely.

> It suited me because I had a big family and the hours didn't interrupt my family life. I was still able to provide for all my children – they were at school when I started but when I left they were all working. Just a few minutes walk.

The lates (12.45 p.m. to 9 or 9.30 p.m.) were not quite as popular as the earlies (7.45 a.m. to 4.30 p.m.).

> I mean a quarter to one was a terrible time to start. It was too early to have lunch: you didn't have no lunch-break then. You didn't have no main meal till seven o'clock in the evening. I left here about half past eleven. It was a horrible shift – I *never* did a late Sunday, the family would have had no Sunday dinner.

But whatever it was, people managed. The telephone switch-board had to be manned all round the clock. The two day-time telephonists – like Jack Spratt and his wife – divided the day in a way that suited them both:

Sunday started our week. I done seven till half-past two. I don't like late night work. I wouldn't go out in the evenings once it was dark, you see. It means I had to get up early, because I had to get the 6.20 bus from here – and I was in there by quarter to seven.

I loved the hours (2.30 p.m. to 9.30 p.m. six days a week) and the reason I loved them was I'm not very good at getting up. I wouldn't like to do anything that meant, you know, I was up early in the morning. So, if I had a lay-in until 11 o'clock I didn't have to get there until half past two. It was lovely.

Night work had few of these attractions. Mrs Hunt was the third telephonist. She had worked consistently on nights on a three-day cycle from 1970 until the closure: on day one she worked from 9 p.m. to 6 a.m., on day two from 10 p.m. to 7 a.m., with the third day off.

It was a *tiring* job, but I was here to put my kids out to school and the main thing was, I was here when they came home. I usually had about five hours sleep a day, which wasn't enough really. I used to get up and go to work and sometimes my bones used to feel a thousand years old. But it used to work off – it always seems to wear off after midnight. Sometimes you'd be walking along and the sun'd be shining, and you just couldn't see people. I used to walk as if I was in a trance. It was just tiredness.

When I was on 9 to 6 and the kids were in school – they used to go into school at ten to nine – I used to do a quick tidy up down here, take what I wanted out for dinner and get into bed by half-past nine. And I used to be up at about two o'clock, and they'd be in at half-past three. Then I'd cook them their evening meal and *then* I'd sit there in the armchair and I was always asleep.

Previously Mrs Green had worked on nights at another hospital but this had been worse because she did not get home until

8.30 in the morning and her husband occasionally failed to get the children off to school. The shift pattern at the hospital allowed her to arrive home just that little bit earlier, in time for the children. The strain eventually made her change to days but by then the habits of night work had been thoroughly implanted. 'I just could not get used to them days – no way. I asked them if there was a vacancy, and I went back on nights.'

To compensate for the disadvantages of nights there was a special camaraderie. Hierarchy was largely forgotten.

We wasn't popular at *all* because they thought we got away with it easy of a night-time. Just because we had no supervision, *they* didn't like it, the day-staff. So it was always, 'Oh, them night-staff!' We called each other by first names. We was just twelve or fourteen friends together. We had a fantastic relationship. There was four of us where I was – Sister, Staff-Nurse, a Pupil, and me – and we had coffee together, we had our meals together, we worked together.

When the closure finally took effect it was not at all like the last day at Fords. An ordinary leaving party was rejected as 'too heartbreaking', but in keeping with the hospital's traditions a memorial service was held in the Chapel and all present and many past staff were invited back to a 'glorified garden party' in the grounds. An exhibition of old and new photographs was mounted and opened to the public. There was a boat trip for nursing staff, distribution of collections of photos and mementoes, and the domestics clubbed together for 'a lovely do at the Admiral'. The Admiral was a local pub. Yet they all had the feeling that it wasn't enough; perhaps under the circumstances nothing could have been. There was still a last day to face. 'On the last day I just went in as usual and just came home. No one to say goodbye to you, to say "It's the last time". Nothing. It was very, very bad. Very, very bad.'

Mrs Palphramand had worked for just twelve hours a week at the hospital but was staggered at the closure and tried to soften the blow by going on working after the end.

In fact I went in voluntary, for two weeks after, helping to clear up. No, I wouldn't go on holiday because we always go in August, and with the hospital closing in July, it was turn and twist whether it was closing or not. We heard on 10 June and up till then there was still a hope. So I couldn't book a holiday. I couldn't take a holiday that year. I couldn't content myself to go until I knew what was happening.

For another woman staying on did help: 'I'm glad I stayed on, though. I'm glad I didn't have to cut myself off completely on that July 10th. I was glad I was able to do it gradually.'

At almost every interview photographs and press-cuttings were brought out showing royal visits, successive nativity tableaux, the attendance of staff at a royal garden party, portraits of the last matron, tea-sets with the name stamped on the pot, letters from patients, a china figure rescued from the chapel before it had been destroyed.

I miss it. Oh yes. Oh yes. The company and the money. I'm not saying I don't because I do. It did get you away and you kept on meeting people. Whereas now you don't.

The same time I finished my son got married and my daughter got married. I was sort of left. I've got time on my hands now. I've got the dog which my daughter bought me when I packed up. She said 'You've got to have some company when Dad's out'. So I take her for walks when I probably wouldn't go out otherwise. That's something.

The most extreme expression of loss came from one woman who described the closure as worse than the loss of her husband. 'It really was the end of my life. Well, I got used to it, I suppose. We all did. At first, when you can't get a job and everything, you feel as if you've been thrown in the dustbin. It's *bad*.'

Life after the death

There is very little to say about what the women did after the closure. The main reason is that they themselves had so much more to say about their time at the hospital than they did about their current lives, and wanted to say it and go on saying it. In this case the long arm of the job reached out in a different way from Fords, gripping the women and facing them back where they had come from. One year on, some still went back to look at what was left of the buildings, mourning their vandalisation and hoping that they might re-open in another form, perhaps even with jobs on offer again. They seized on any hint that life might return to the place: 'That's why I wonder if it would re-open. There was a lot of rumours. I was quite prepared to do anything, go back to *any* hours. We kept on saying "Perhaps we'll get a job there. There's bound to be a cafeteria." I don't mind doing that again.'

It was clear that by and large the women who had families gradually became more absorbed in them. Instead of the home improvements which fell to the men they started out on major spring-cleans. They did more of what they had never completely given up and sometimes they began rather tentatively to form what could be thought of as a 'new life'. Like Mrs French:

I was lucky in a way. My husband was made redundant three weeks after me. That helped a lot because we were able to do things together. We joined the library and go there twice a week. We've got the car and we have had little runs into the country. Every Monday I go and clean up for my 99-year-old neighbour. Then one day a week I go to one of my married sons and while my daughter-in-law does the washing I do the ironing for her. So that's like two days a week really. The winter's over now and we've got a nice little routine. But you know I picked up the phone – you wouldn't believe this – but I saw a number to ring for auxiliaries wanted and I picked up the phone on Monday and I phoned.

But even the intensification of the domestic round could not always compensate.

My son and daughter's just come back from holiday. They were away for a fortnight and a weekend, and it felt like six months. Normally when I'm working and they've gone like that I am quite happy. But I was bored stiff, it was terrible. In fact, one weekend I rang up my daughter and asked if I could borrow her kids. I haven't taken up anything new. Nothing to take up really, is there?

The busy routine of the two jobs, one paid, the other not, had been grievously disrupted and for the time being there was nothing to take its place.

Then I started to get bored. I got everything sorted out and straight, the carpets cleaned, everything. The days seem to go ever so quick. I find it's the night that drags, from after tea-time . . . I don't go around in other people's houses. I don't believe in having neighbours in and out. Nobody ever comes in here; I'm not one of them. I want to be doing something, not sitting gossiping. My life has always been like that.

Some of the markers could still be held on to. 'I used to go shopping every Thursday – funnily enough it's still a Thursday. You used to get paid on a Thursday, it was weekly.'
One unusual woman was happy enough with her retirement and thought anyone could be 'if you've got some interests'. She was now able to join in activities she used to have less time for when working – swimming, guiding and the local antiquarian society. But there was no sense of having stepped purposefully over the threshold into retirement, only an acceptance that a critical point had been passed and survived. 'As I say, I was sixty-six, so really I was retiring. And my husband had retired by then, so we just *retired*. That was it, so there you are.'

*   *   *

Both sets of workers show how much work matters and therefore how difficult it is to grasp the new freedom, and how easily the second age can colour the third and determine whether people can take the decisive step of entering into the third age at all. Every one of the people we shall be citing from now on has as much of a history behind them as the engineers or the auxiliary nurses and ancillary staff. We would say that by and large the Ford men were in the third age, mostly in the positive form of it, because their work had put them there. Their jobs had been very demanding and could be undermining to their health. Several of them had noticed the ageing effect of their gruelling work – as work becomes less strenuous this itself should give people a better chance of enjoying their third age. If they had not left early, some of the Ford men thought they might never have made it into such a new phase of life; by sixty-five they might have been 'worn out', a human machine that needed the replacement it would not get. As it was, retiring with their capacities pretty much intact gave them a chance to build a new life or at least to enjoy what they had, even if it was not exactly new. They were reacting against the work they had done and its monotony without having been incapacitated by it.

Contentment is a matter of comparison, and so the Ford men did not need to be doing anything very new or stretching themselves unduly in order to feel content. They had only to summon up the past in order to show themselves, and us, how fortunate they were. Jack Walters was able to give himself 'little injections of happiness' by remembering how grim it *had* been. The men were happy because they had not been happy in the same way before, and perhaps all the more so because many years of toil had given them such an unchallengeable entitlement to their new state. Far from feeling guilty, they could – with some self-satisfaction – feel that they deserved the present they were now enjoying. In so far as life was monotonous, at least it was not made monotonous by someone else, and for some of them, like Eric Tanner, it was not in the least monotonous – far from it. If people who want to retire (or make any sharp change in their lives) have two main motives, the push motive which inclines them away from what they have not liked, and the pull motive which draws them to something they hope to like, for the Ford men the push motive must be reckoned the most important. They appreciated the 'freedom from' of their lives – the freedom from work – so much that it gave them a good start towards turning 'freedom from' into 'freedom to'. They had also earned enough money in wages to allow them to accumulate some private capital and had enough income after retirement to keep money worries at bay.

The Maternity Hospital was different. The people did not have so much to say about their lives after the closure but from what they did say it was clear enough they were not contented. The comparison they made with their past work led them to the opposite conclusion. The women were unhappy partly because they had been so happy, in a job which was the site of daily miracles to which they were contributory, which gave them a chance to meet lots of people, where there was a remarkable camaraderie, in a place held in such high regard locally and where, as part-timers, they had 'lovely hours' which allowed them to combine their home families with their work families without sacrificing either. They show how wrong is 'the common assumption that retirement from paid employment is "far less drastic" for women than for men. The majority of women do undertake paid work in their later middle life, and it can be just as wrenching for them to leave it as for men'.* By and large the attitudes of the hospital workers were not those of the third age, and this even though they had been part-timers. Even if they did not have jobs, they have to be considered second agers.

The lesson to be drawn from the two case-studies was that any decent dispensation needs somehow to allow for both sorts of people in both sorts of jobs. The Ford workers benefited from retiring early, and millions would do the same. The hospital workers did not want to retire at all, and millions more would be like them. The problem for policy is how to face opposite ways without letting one line of sight exclude the other.

* P. Thompson, C. Itzin and M. Abendstern, *I Don't Feel Old – The Experience of Later Life*, p.8.

THREE

The Age Trap

'I'm not a person. For years the government's
got you in a position where you don't exist.'
Mr Wylde, Greenwich

Between them the factory and the hospital highlighted two of
this book's key questions. How many people in our sample were
like the hospital workers in remaining attached to the particular
jobs they had before, or wanting paid work for other reasons?
That is the question for this chapter. If they were attached, we
considered them as still belonging to the second age. We shall
go on in later chapters to those who were no longer in the grip
of ordinary work and ask how many of them had in fact made
it into a third age of the positive sort.

We take separately the unemployed who were still seeking
work and the retired who were no longer job hunting, and divide
the retired further into the medically retired, the early retired
and the normally retired.* Their numbers are in the table.

Numbers unemployed and retired

	MEN	WOMEN	TOTAL
Unemployed	26	5	31
Medically Retired	19	5	24
Early Retired	37	15	52
Normally Retired	22	20	42
TOTALS	104	45	149

* A category (which we have tried to allow for in a different way) of 'discour-
aged' people who were not looking for work because they believed no jobs to
be available was identified by B. Casey and F. Laczko, 'Early Retired or Long-
Term Unemployed'.

The unemployed were selected by a more stringent test than the government's. More of our sample – fifty-four people – told us they were registered as unemployed with the Department of Employment than were counted as such by us. This was because we did not consider anyone as unemployed unless they definitely wanted to find another job, and some of them who were registered did not. The Ford workers, and those like them, did not. They registered in order to secure the year's unemployment benefit they had a right to as part of an early retirement package. Others had given up on the search for jobs because they did not think there were any to get. People over sixty were particularly apt to do this because they knew that in the ordinary way they would be turned down by reason of their age alone. They were registered, but they were no longer in the job market. The government itself accepted that they were in a special situation, allowing (even encouraging) them to receive supplementary benefit at what used to be a higher rate while removing them from the official unemployment register.

Hope sinks eternal

Whatever their occupation had been, almost all these people were set back by losing it – particularly if the loss was not something repetition had accustomed them to, or they had never experienced it before. For one man dismissal felt 'like being cut by a knife', for another 'like a ship going down'. For Mr Little the shock came a little later when he went to the official Job Centre whose responsibility is to help people get jobs. 'When the man behind the desk saw my age, fifty-nine, he said "You don't stand an earthly of getting a job". I could have burst into tears.'

Most of those to whom it had happened before started off, like Mr Little, by being hopeful. Having lost their job many times and always so far found another, they thought it would be the same again. Mr Earle expected he would be able to do so 'in the old way'. With his hernia and weak back he could not do the heavy work he had done before but short of that he was ready for almost anything. He could not believe he would not impress some employer with his experience and his keenness. He applied to hundreds of advertisements, made hundreds of telephone calls and turned up in dozens of offices but to no avail. Others equally determined did not get on their bikes but walked and walked, as one of them said, 'from one side of London to the other, looking for work'. Their fatiguing and dispiriting work was looking for work.

Most of those who started off by being choosy, keen to find a job at least as good as before, gradually lowered their sights. Mr Trimmer was a specialised crane driver and steel erector for constructing power stations and through his own grapevine knew about any new power station contracts that were going anywhere in the country. He was prepared to go anywhere and live anywhere and would travel to sites all over the country to put himself forward. In the past he had nearly always got another job within a fortnight of ending an old one. He knew it would be harder this time but not nearly as hard as it proved to be. Even when he had almost persuaded himself to give up hope and the pain that hope brought, the merest hint of an opening was still enough to revive it: three days previously he had driven to Southampton for a crane-driving job which turned out to have already gone to someone else. His savings were a growing worry. He had £3,000 when his last job packed up. At first he spent at about the same rate as when he had been earning, expecting that he would soon be able to make it up. With each major setback he adjusted his expenditure and his expectations downwards, always fearing he might not have been savage enough with himself. By the time of the interview he could not go much lower. He only had £130 to go. He was left with an even more formidable problem: with all his savings gone, how was he going to live on unemployment benefit which to him seemed pitiably little and likely to remain at that pitiable level?

Mr Philpott had been slipping down the occupational ladder for some time, and also lowering his expectations step by step. He had gone from more to less secure jobs, being the victim of the 'last in, first out' custom which protects the longer-serving. He had not been overjoyed when the only job he could get was as a labourer for a printer who had exploited him mercilessly; he only stuck it because he feared other devils might be even worse. After he was sacked he eventually managed to get another job, sweeping up the leaves in Greenwich Park. It brought less money and less status. But he liked it much better. There was no boss to harry him; he was out in the open and on his own. He started work in September, the falling leaves giving him his work. By January the trees were bare, the leaves all burnt. With them went his job, and he did not now expect such luck, or any luck, again. It was going to remain winter.

Mr Spice was a skilled welder. The job was always varied, always interesting. He tried for another one in his own trade and, failing in that, moved sideways or downwards to another as an office cleaner. He clung to that for three years, as diligent about the cleaning as he had been about the welding – 'it was better than nothing' – until he was again made redundant. Being that much older he had now given up hope, or tried to, although of course if something did actually turn up . . .

Mr Pollitt, one of the council tenants, was almost a walking history of redundancy. He could have offered himself for a life study at a business school. He left ordinary school at fourteen and went to work in an engineering factory as an apprentice. But his study days ended in 1939 when his night school was taken over by the Auxiliary Fire Service and the local air-raid wardens. In 1940 he joined the RAF and returned to Siemens (the engineers) in 1946. He was an assistant foreman when Amalgamated Engineering Industries, as Siemens had by then become, closed down in 1968. He moved to a high-tech American firm, which fairly soon decamped to Glenrothes in Scotland. He then got a job at another engineer's in Deptford where he worked for eleven and a half years as a Senior Inspector. In 1982 he was made redundant shortly after the firm had closed its Deptford plant and moved him to Lewisham. Five weeks later he got a job, to use his words, 'in an absolutely Dickensian firm'. It was an old metal-bashing company which amazingly still made high quality products – for instance, they did seventy separate jobs for Rolls-Royce on their trim-line as well as many for more down-market cars like Vauxhall and Ford. They also made metal shelving and trolley wheels. Mr Pollitt showed us a length of metal strip which they had 'extruded', that is spun off a metal coil, up to a length of twenty-four feet – exceptional even today.

The majority of lengths were twelve to eighteen feet and were produced by 'some poor semi-literate devil running out from the coil until told to stop'. The order to run was given by the old boss who would cut the length himself. Lighting and heating were kept to a very bare minimum. When a hot tap was left running one night the boss took the tops off all the taps so there was no hot water at all. That job did not last long either. When the factory closed all Mr Pollitt got was two weeks' holiday.

The only pension he had from any of his jobs was frozen so he could not touch it before he was sixty-five. He did not get a State pension at his age (sixty-one), nor did his wife. He had accumulated about £3,000 in lump sum redundancy payments.

You can survive provided you don't want hair-cuts or new shoes. I walk over to Deptford to get a hair-cut for £1.80 because up at Blackheath you can't get one under £2.20. We're not paupers you understand. There's a lot much worse off than we are. We've always given our elder son some money.

The elder son was a monk living near Brighton. Mr Pollitt desperately wanted to work again but only because, the official retirement age being sixty-five, he thought he could not count himself as retired. Reducing the retirement age would have removed or reduced his guilt and allowed him and his wife to plan a new future for themselves.

In the block of flats where they lived he used to remark to his wife that they were one of only two households that were paying full rent and rates, most of the others being pensioners with rebates. He didn't resent their privilege. Of his job search he said: 'If I don't go to the Job Centre I feel guilty. If I do, I feel depressed.' He still went once or twice a week and had applied for over twenty jobs in the last months. Usually it was age that ruled him out – no one over fifty (he had been told this so often he made a sing-song out of it – 'no one over fifty') need apply. He applied for warehouse jobs, driving jobs, labouring jobs and even went for a car-cleaning job up the Old Kent Road. Always being turned down but without self-pity.

In some respects I am lucky. We've only got to struggle through these next few years and then we shall know where we are and I could perhaps get a part-time job then. I did contemplate using some of our money to buy a new car and go cabbying but I don't think I could drive fast enough. It's mainly not knowing that causes the problems.

For him free time was a punishment.

We revisited Mr Pollitt two years later. He was still looking for work, and still, in his own words, 'in limbo'. Housing was for him and his wife a current concern that stemmed from a long way back. They had lined up an exchange of flats with a family in Brighton but this had fallen through after they had spent money on a gas fire and a bigger carpet for the new place. They felt keenly about not having their own house.

Obviously we were working class. I feel that we would have had a lot higher opinion of ourselves if we'd had our own property. I had six uncles: five of them had their own houses. The deposit on them was £25; that was about two to three months' wages. The houses were about £250 each. Now what would you need to put down a deposit?

He felt caged in a council flat.

Larry over the way there. He retired last year, now he's gone from snuff to smoking. He says it relaxes him. I prowl from this window to the kitchen and I know he does the same because I see him there. I'm really amazed: they keep saying, 'There's too many retired people'. I think, well what are they saying, should we feel guilty about living?

Such people were driven not only by money but by shame. The stigma was repeatedly reinforced by their compulsory attendance at the 'shaming ceremony' at the Department of Employment office where they had to demonstrate, by signing on, their desire for the work they could not get. No one had a good word for the staff there. 'No one', remarked Mr Earle, 'says "hello" at the Department of Employment. It'll be a celebration day all right when I don't have to sign on any more.'

The discourtesy hurt more because the clerks were so young. They made Mr Philpott feel even older than his age by being so young he could easily be their father.

Age was drummed into them. They were always asked how old they were when applying for a job, and whatever they replied they were nearly always told that if that's how old they were they were *too* old. It was a cumulative humiliation. Too old at fifty or fifty-five, some of them felt they would have been too old at forty, even at thirty-five. 'The minute you say your age they don't want to know.' Mr Macadam said bitterly, 'They're looking for eighteen-plus but the plus soon stops.' Since for employers age was already such a barrier, our informants also expected it was bound to get more so. If suffering from lack of esteem now, they would suffer from it still more in the future. They would be older and there would be a longer period of unemployment to count against them, and to account for, since they last had a job at all. Time in making them older would stretch out the rack continuously, which is good reason for having a law against age-discrimination. We shall come back to this issue in the final chapter.

The State and employers between them have been putting people like these in a double bind. On the one hand it is dinned into them by employers that they are too old; on the other, they are told by the State that they are not old enough. They are in what we have thought of as the Age Trap. The length of life and the length of work have moved in opposite directions, opening up a gap into which many fall. For many employers, old age may start at fifty, or even before that; for the State it does not, as we stressed in the opening chapter, start until sixty for women and sixty-five for men, precisely. Many men felt the unfairness of it. Instead of blaming employers, they tended to blame the State for not adjusting downwards its official reckoning of age in accordance with the changing situation in the labour market. The government, as one of them said, was turning the vice to squeeze people out of existence. At sixty Mr Wheale said he felt he had to work but couldn't. 'I don't think I'll live to sixty-five if I go on like this. I can't tell my wife. It's such a long time to hang on, five years, to get to sixty-five and the State pension. If the pension age came down it might be better, it's a matter of ego.' Mr Groom was almost equally unhappy at what he called the in-between place he was in. 'You can't call yourself a pensioner and join the club. It's an in-between status.' At the age of sixty-three Mr Earle (who will reappear later) was trying out a unilateral declaration of independence from the tyranny. If the State would not do it he had decided to call himself 'retired' and relax. But he could not quite pull it off. It was a 'bit of a white lie': if a suitable job came along he would have returned like a shot from retirement. In the interview he tried out on us a brand-new description of himself, 'semi-retired'. But he was too hesitant even about that; he could not kid himself that he did not still want work.

Mr Groom was not alone in resenting the fact that, while too old in the employer's office, as soon as he and his like got out of it they were not old enough for a free NHS prescription from their doctor, for a bus or tube pass from London Transport, for a senior citizen's concession on British Rail, for a pensioner's lunch club, or for Meals on Wheels and Home Helps, for sheltered housing if that's what they wanted or for a half-price ticket as senior citizens at the Greenwich Observatory or the cinema. They suffered the indignity of being called 'Dad' or 'Grandad' without any of Dad's or Grandad's rights. They were stuck in an Age Trap such that their age debarred them from both job and pension just as people are stuck in a Poverty Trap when they reduce their income if they get a job. The Age Trap is a pit whose width is the number of years between becoming unemployed and getting the pension; it is a hole that its victims are dropped into by their age to become a kind of non-person while they are there. The trap is dug so deep that once caught, few can clamber up one side of it to rejoin the people of their own age who have jobs, and no one can climb up the other side until they are of pensionable age.

The five unemployed women had an alternative role to retreat into. The alternative can prevent the desolation which confronts unemployed men who have never learnt to work in the house, or who, to their own cost, devalue it as not really being work at all. But unemployment could still be painful. Mrs Defoe was not registered as unemployed. She had returned from Singapore because her husband's contract there had come to an end. She gave up her own job as a bleep controller in a business communications company and came back home with him. They were then both unemployed until he got a job as a maintenance engineer. Mrs Defoe looked after someone else's child, from 6.30 a.m. to 5 p.m., and although she got paid she did not see it as a job and the income was not declared. She wanted 'real' paid work outside the house which is why we counted her unemployed, despite the pay. At the age of fifty she saw herself as obsolescent. Her confidence had evaporated. Mrs Defoe was left, uncertainly and unwillingly combining paid and unpaid domestic work.

Mrs Brace's last job had been barmaid in a social club. She was squeezed out to make way for a friend of the manageress. Though a step down from her previous work as a self-employed interior decorator she had enjoyed it. It gave her social contacts, money, a sense of worth and a structure to her day. She had never had a career like her professional husband. Two of her four children were still at home. But work mattered to her, and its absence was a major blow. Not having it had meant cutting back on social activities, and she surprised us by saying she had had to give up Ascot, the opera and dinner parties. She also felt more of a drudge at home.

> Going out to work is much easier than staying at home. Your life is far more clearly defined and you're not so much at everyone's beck and call. Here everyone says 'Oh she's not working, she can do such and such'. Particularly it's my husband's attitude: if things went wrong and you were working it was excusable, but if you weren't he just couldn't understand that not having a job can be as much of a strain and as tiring as a full-time job.

Unlike Mrs Brace, most unemployed people certainly had leisure. But they had too much, whereas other people did not have enough. Their compulsory leisure was too often spoiled by lack of the money which would have allowed them to enjoy it more and to feel they had the right to do so. They belonged to the world of work and yet were rejected by it. They had to bear both poverty and a sense of shame for not being able to get the work that would relieve it, and all because of their age which they were not allowed to forget. Some of them had little hope that they would ever again be able to get relief until others regarded them, and they regarded themselves, as retired. We cannot consider them as anything but second agers of a negative sort.

Medically retired

Those who gave poor health as the primary reason for their retirement – and this whether or not they were actually getting disability or invalidity benefit from the State – were in other respects better off. They did not have to feel guilty because they were unemployed or pass themselves off as retired but under false pretences because they were not yet old enough for it. Calling themselves medically retired was a means of avoiding at any rate the psychological injury of the Age Trap. If they received disability or invalidity benefits they were also a little better off in material terms than the unemployed. Low and inadequate though these were, and are, they were not so low as unemployment benefit. 'Invalids' do not have to be penalised for not working, or their income from the dole kept so low that they will welcome any work, almost however badly paid. They were not meant to be able to work and it was not their fault that they could not. To be unable to work was respectable because it was regrettable in a manner for which they did not have to feel responsibility.

Despite their self-definition we did not know whether any of the twenty-four people in this category would have to be ruled out from the third age because even so they hankered so strongly for a job. A few were certainly sorry to have lost theirs. Mr Warburg, for example, had been a police constable for twenty-eight years. Policemen usually retired at fifty but he had not, or not totally: he had become a Gateman at Buckingham Palace, opening and closing the gates for the Queen and other members of the Royal Family and for visiting dignitaries, and doing it with the utmost punctiliousness. 'The Queen arrives at Admiralty Arch at a precise time and I had to be all ready to open the gates at a precise time so many seconds later.' He had no wish whatever to leave. He was very proud of the job. But when he was sixty he developed a tremble in his hands and he feared that people watching him tremblingly fumble with the massive iron gates would say, 'What kind of a policeman is that with his shaking hands?' The only decent thing he could do was retire early. He did so with a bang. As the last in a long line, he was interviewed on television on his final day at the Palace. For when he left, the specialist post of Royal Gateman was also abolished – contradicting the general rule of growing specialisation. Even if the job had not disappeared he would not have thought himself fit enough to do it justice.

Others who had also been fond of their jobs had put the idea of having one out of their minds. Mrs Durr had been a hairdresser. She wanted to do it as a child and it had never lost its appeal. She could not see hair on a person, or on a dog or cat for that matter, without wanting to clip it off or into shape. But the best thing for her was the ease with which people talked to her and she could talk to them while they were in the chair under her hands. 'The advice I could give, the advice I was given, how they cooked, how they did their knitting, where they travelled. It's marvellous what you can learn. It makes you happy.' Then she was struck down by a run of misfortunes like the plagues in Egypt. She had a toe off and got gangrene, went down with diabetes, broke five ribs, lost the sight of one eye, and had three slipped discs. After that she could carry on her delightful work only in one way, by cutting as often as possible the hair of other disabled people for nothing. She turned herself into a volunteer, but still a professional.

Mr Salmon had had to give up his job as a chauffeur because he contracted Paget's Disease. There was no cure and it was leaving him more and more incapacitated as time went on. He had been officially classed as disabled and that gave him a sense of security of a kind. He was not indeterminate like some other people, perhaps being 'unemployed', perhaps being 'ill', perhaps being 'retired'. The official designation made him willing to accept that he could properly be dependent on the welfare state in a way which otherwise he would have loathed. He comforted himself that the words which his father had drilled into his mind – 'If you don't work, you can't eat' – did not apply to him because he couldn't work. He had changed it into 'if you can't work, you can eat.'

He also made light of having to give up work. Other events in his life had been so much more traumatic – his father's death, the break-up of his first marriage, serious illnesses. He said he was perfectly content to sit on the balcony of his flat and 'watch the world go by'. The world might consist for the most part of a few children too young for school, shouting and tearing up and down the stairs by his balcony. But seeing them, he could draw the customary comfort from the customary cliché.

Mr Urwin, also let down by his health, had not taken it so well. There was a bitter twist to his mouth. He had put all he had into every job that he'd done, and now felt poorly rewarded. 'When I look back I think what a fool I was – how naïve, allowing myself to be used: on the cable ship, at the Funnel, at Barkers.' His resentment sparked off a series of broadsides: at his various employers; at his own ill-health with what breath emphysema left him; at the Labour Party for betraying its and his values; and at Mrs Thatcher for destroying the manufacturing base of the country and his job in it, and also the country's crowning glory, the National Health Service.

His misfortunes had not been spread out any more than Mrs Durr's had. He had collapsed the previous August with a heart attack and been rushed to the intensive care unit. A week later he was told he would never work again. A long period of convalescence followed. In the middle of it he drove to his old workplace to say goodbye. On the way back a lorry jumped the lights and smashed into him. To replace the car cost him most of his lump-sum compensation. Two months before, his thirty-year-old son had been involved in a motorbike accident, and was now living with him whilst his leg mended – except that it wasn't knitting and would probably have to be broken again. A neighbour passed as we stood at his garden gate.

'All right, George?'
'All right.'
'How's Kevin?'
'He's doing all right.'
'Leg's getting better then?'
'Yes – well actually they say it may not be knitting.'

The most important thing in his life had been the Royal Marines. As a Marine he had been decorated for bravery. A major factor in helping him to fight depression was the re-forming of his old unit. He was asked to visit its commander and invited to the relaunch ceremony. He went up to London specially to get his medals properly prepared and then travelled painfully down to Portsmouth. He and his son were the only civilians there. The general came across the parade ground and saluted him. 'My hand was half-way up to my head – I didn't know what to do.' He was presented with a plaque which he mounted on his wall when he got home. And he was asked to be the surprise guest of honour at an old comrade's fortieth wedding anniversary. The occasion was a wonderful blend of tears and laughter.

His career after leaving the Royal Marines had been flawed by his lack of formal training. On the cable ship where he worked at first he was responsible for X-raying the booster fittings which were put down every few miles to join together two lengths of the submarine cable. His task was to take the appliance and X-ray the cable from several angles to see if there were any 'voids'.

> I got it down to four minutes: taking three pictures, dashing down to the dark-room, processing the pictures, back up on deck. 'OK lads, carry on'. . . . I was only a Seaman Cablehand and my grade was never changed though I was wholly responsible. Most radiographers had been to college, and you can't cross that line.

His second job was with Funnel Refineries working with starch powder. He became the factory shift foreman. 'The shift I had, I'm proud to say, had the best record but it didn't make any difference when they cut down.' The numbers of foremen were reduced from fourteen to two. There followed five months out of work. He made strenuous efforts to get a job. 'I even tried across the water, at the London Rubber Company.' Being prepared to cross the Thames showed his eagerness.

Eventually he did get another job at a factory making empty cardboard boxes in Deptford, a subsidiary of Barker International. He learnt how to do it from the works manager who had forty years' experience. When he died suddenly Mr Urwin took over as manager. He had mixed feelings. On the one hand he had always been the one to fill a vacuum by taking charge. On the other hand he was inhibited by his lack of education.

> I couldn't shut the door and forget the job. It was a little bit of inferiority because I didn't have the qualifications. So I had to prove myself. I always used to get there half an hour early, first in, last to go.

He was free to come and go, take time off when he wanted. But 'I don't think anyone's ever really a master of their time. There are two schools of thought: those who believe you make your own life and those who think life is mostly what other people make for you.' Mr Urwin classified himself as one of the latter.

After ten years with Barkers he was made redundant. He was then fifty-six, and realised his chances of another job like that were slim. So he took the first one he could get – sweeping the floor at a Territorial Army Depot. He did that for eighteen months, very boring work, before they made him storeman. The paperwork was all routine, but he took it very seriously.

> The store job suited someone of my age. A younger person wouldn't stand the pace. Not that it was fast, but it needed discipline. I got engrossed even in this job. The chap next to me used to chat a bit and I had to tell him to shut up.

The end came when he fainted in the storeroom of which he had become so fond.

But although Mr Urwin was a man who needed work, he had accepted he would not get it again, and he was making the best of looking after the house. The fixed point in the day was 5.20 p.m. when he took the car down to the station to pick up his wife who was still working. The evening started a little before that, at 4 p.m., when he began to prepare the dinner which he had never done before when they were both working. Saturday was shopping day: arduous, because he had difficulty in walking and she could not carry much because of an arthritic arm. His face was resigned, but there was still the odd flash of animation as he got into the swing of a story about his past in the Marines. The past was a resource for him to draw on, even if the future was blank.

The other medically retired people were not unlike Mr Urwin, although some were finding it even more difficult to cope. Mr Wilson was one of those managing less well. He was classed as disabled, though not perhaps irretrievably, because of his addiction to alcohol. A self-made career man, he had at one stage been managing director of a factory in Essex making elastic thread, with a substantial budget under his control. Divorce and drink had reduced him to a council flat in Plumstead and a thoroughly mundane job with Westminster City Council. While he still had that job he and his second wife, also an alcoholic, had with the support of Alcoholics Anonymous managed quite well. But their carefully organised arrangements fell to pieces when their working schedules were changed, particularly when his wife, who was a nurse, started working evenings and nights. In the mornings he might manage to avoid nipping into the off-licence at Waterloo Station as its first customer; but when he got home at the end of the day and she was out in her hospital he would find himself with nothing to do. The pub beckoned. It was too much of a temptation not to spend two or three hours there and bring back a bottle of vodka to keep himself going. When he missed going to the office too often he was retired by the Council on 'health grounds'. But he had not given up completely, nor had his wife. At the time of the interview the two of them were about to celebrate one month off drink, that is one month since his 'birthday', which the AA regards as the day an alcoholic stops drinking. During that month he had been called to a selection committee for another job. He was very keen to get it; they were both optimistic. But when we returned to pick up the diary, his wife was distraught. He was sprawled in the bedroom with an empty vodka bottle beside him.

Mr Wilson apart, we have seen that the kind of ill-health suffered by people who had retired on these grounds was itself reason enough for them not to be counted as in the second age. They were 'free' from the hold of work, even though they were not free from the limitations imposed on them by their health,

and when they were managing, as many of them were remark-
ably well, they could only do so within their limitations. But
whatever their condition, it did not rule them out from a positive
third age.

Early retirement

The fifty-two early retired* were all people not in the unemployed category who left work *before* the normal ages of retirement set by the State *or*, if it was sooner than that, before the
standard age set by their employer.** None of them disqualified
themselves from the third age by their attachment to the second.

For some it was quite clear how this had happened. They had
chosen to retire early in rather the way the Ford workers had,
but mostly without so much financial advantage. One of the
commonest motives was to be with a wife or a husband who
needed the company or the care. Mrs Moseley was not unhappy
to pull out: she had not been getting on with a newly appointed
manageress in her office. But the more important reason was
that her husband was retiring and she did not want to leave him
at home on his own. It was the same with Mrs Clough, except
that she had delayed her decision. Her husband had retired three
years previously. As a substitute for herself she had at that time
bought him a dog 'to make sure he got out of the house'. But

---

* A study made for the EEC defined early retirement or *pré-retraite* in this
way: 'The early retired are those who have left the labour market for good,
before retirement age, by virtue of an economic or an employment policy.'
Hannelore Jani-Le Bris, '*L'Insertion Sociale des Préretraités* (EEC, 1988), p.6.
According to our criteria, a person has retired early because he or she has to,
or is given the chance to, by 'an economic or an employment policy'; or
because he or she chooses to whether there is such a policy or not. The EEC
study confined itself to a study of the effects of government and employer
policy and that we did not do. For a general discussion see S. Parker, *Work
and Retirement*, pp.89–90.
** 'Early' is therefore judged by its relationship to a norm in a particular
context. An 'early grandmother' amongst black people of Los Angeles is someone who has grandchildren before thirty-five; after that you are 'on time', up
to the point in your forties when you become a 'late' grandmother; see V.L.
Bengston, 'Sociological perspectives on aging, families and the future'.

he had not managed to adjust even with the help of the dog and his boredom was turning into depression. So although she was a 'bit choked' at leaving her work she had done so to be with him. By contrast, Mrs Douglas was really glad to go. Knowing when her husband was to retire, she did so herself a few months beforehand to get everything ready for him. Even before that she had begun stocking up on major household equipment like a washing machine because they might never be able to afford to do so again. It was her last fling in the consumer society. She had planned it all in great detail and had enjoyed it. It was as though she was taking in stores against a siege that was going to last the rest of their lifetimes. Mrs Straight retired in order to look after not her husband but her ninety-year-old mother who was needing more and more attention.

Needless to say, it was not only women who retired on such indirect health grounds, that is not on account of their own health but of someone else's.* Mr Macadam, for instance, wanted to look after his wife. He was a highly determined man who prided himself on his own independence. Once before when his wife had a serious operation he took over and, without heeding the medical staff, wheeled her out of hospital in the conviction that she would do better at home with him looking after her than staying in the hospital cared for by the nurses. Now that she was poorly again he had no doubt that he should retire to be with her. He hoped she would be well enough to fly out with him to Australia to see their son before they settled down together at home, with himself in the caring role which came so easily to him.

The other most common reason was not that people pulled out voluntarily but that they had to because of changes in the nature of their work. Mr Hastings, for example, was a photo-printer technician responsible for the production of microfilms. Until recently he had been in charge of quality control but a reorganisation of the system and the introduction of more modern equipment both reduced the extent of his responsibility

---

* See S. Arber and N. Gilbert, 'Transitions in Caring: gender, life course and the care of the elderly'. Arber and Gilbert confirmed that it was mostly women who did the caring; nevertheless about one third of carers were men.

and speeded up his rate of work. Each day he had felt that he was working against the clock and his response was to 'clock off' mentally. Relations with the boss grew more and more strained. At the age of sixty-two – three years before the retirement age that was his employer's as well as the State's – he was, as the boss put it, 'given' early retirement which, despite everything, he still did not want.

Mr Kermode had worked for twenty-eight years as a machine operator at an engineering factory. It had been a family firm. It was taken over and the level of investment was cut down. Mr Kermode did not like working with out-of-date equipment. For Mrs Macauley it was the opposite problem of too much investment or, at any rate, of new machinery that was very different from what she had been used to. She was employed in the traditional Greenwich industry of rope-making. The new machines made the work less laborious but also less convivial and far more boring. She took early retirement while she could. It was rather the same story with Mr Willis, a draughtsman. The result of a takeover of his firm was 'whizz kids and VDU's all over the place'. He left to get away from them. Mr Daniels was a lecturer in an engineering college. He had been downgraded, teaching young people in the Youth Training Scheme instead of the Diploma-level students he had had before. He also took himself off.

Mrs Thirsk, Mr Trimble and Mr Stephens did not have any element of choice. Mrs Thirsk had been for twelve years manageress of a pub until her fourth child was born. She went back later to work along with her husband to form a two-person toilet-cleaning team for the Council. But after some years the contract was put out to tender and it was won by a private firm who had use only for Mr Thirsk, not for his wife. She was bitter about the discrimination, and especially so against the union, which she considered had not fought for its women members. 'All the women left but the men carried on. They had other jobs for the men, road sweeping and things like that, but nothing for the women.' Mr Trimble had been made redundant from his job as foreman after forty-eight years with the same company. He got generous compensation but was still aggrieved that it had happened when he only had one year to go before his normal retirement. Mr Stephens had worked for his company, building boats, for almost as long, thirty-seven years. For substantial periods he had done overtime, working for up to a hundred hours in a week. He was given two hours' notice when, without any warning, the company closed.

It was just bad management. It was terrible when it happened. I wouldn't have minded retiring or being made redundant in the proper way, but not when the receiver came in. I went to work at eight and was home by one o'clock out of work. We just arrived and found the receiver sitting there.

Painful as early retirement was for some, it certainly was not for others. A far higher proportion of them – about twice as many as in the rest of the sample – reported that it had been their own decision to leave work, and more than twice as many – four out of five compared with one third of the rest – said they now enjoyed life more or much more than when they were working.

Normally retired

Since the circumstances were of the kind we have illustrated, it is hardly surprising that there were no second agers amongst the early retired. This was not so amongst the forty-two normally retired, that is retired at or after the normal age set by their employer or the State. Five of them were classified as second agers. A few of the people we interviewed, although sixty-five or under when the sample was drawn, were over sixty-five when we first saw them.

For the great majority it was all straightforward enough. They had reached the retirement age for their company, expected to leave and did so. Mr Welsh, for example, had worked all his life at the Royal Arsenal as a clerical officer. The standard retirement age was sixty for both men and women, but they were allowed to carry on till sixty-five, subject to an annual review of their competence. He lasted out till sixty-five and thereby completed his fifty years of service with the Arsenal. His wife prepared him for it. 'The wife got me used to it over the two years before. She broke me in gently, helping me to buy spare clothes and so on for the time we would not be able to afford them.' Again, the siege mentality. Mrs Weedon had been works manager of a small factory where the retirement age was sixty-five but people could go at sixty if they wished and Mrs Weedon did. She had planned for it over several years. 'It was a general winding-down, or planned decline.' She spoke about it as if she had read Isaiah Berlin and us. 'All my life I'd been told what to do. You should have freedom from other people and from the clock, and there's no freedom until you retire.'

Sometimes it was more the spouse's expectations that were decisive. Mrs York wanted to carry on working part-time but her husband forbade it. 'He said no, you've done enough.'

Then there were the five who did not conform and came somewhere near bearing out Simone de Beauvoir's description.

> The adult behaves as though he will never grow old. Working men are often amazed, stupefied when the day of their retirement comes. Its date was fixed well beforehand; they knew it; they ought to have been ready for it. In fact, unless they have been thoroughly indoctrinated politically, this knowledge remains entirely outside their ken.*

For our people it seemed to be not so much the fact that they could not accept how old they were as that they could not reconcile themselves to being without work. Mr Wheale could not settle at all. For twenty-seven years he had been a despatch clerk in British Petroleum and had known all that time he would have to retire at sixty. The company could not be faulted, giving him a pre-retirement course and an extra lump sum of £2,000 on top of his entitlement, but all to no avail. He enjoyed his freedom for the first two months; it was like a fine holiday extended longer than he had ever had before. But then he became restless for it to be over so that he could get back into 'harness', if not into BP's harness then someone else's. He began to think

* Simone de Beauvoir, *Old Age*, p.4.

he would not even live to sixty-five, he was so miserable without his harness. If this was freedom it was so disagreeable he thought freedom was killing him.

Mr Montgomery was similar. He had already slid downwards like so many others, in his case from skilled engineer to wire-worker, but that did not make him any the less keen to hang on as tightly as he could. He felt as though he had been forced on to the dole, or as he put it, 'onto the scrapheap'. Mr Barnes was not so affronted. He just did not see any reason why he should not continue working as before. He was in the same excellent health. He could still manage seventy to eighty hours a week as a maintenance engineer. His wife wanted him to stop; but he did not agree and was going to look for work.

Then there was Mr Dobson who had failed to get the money which he needed for the kind of retirement he had planned for himself. He had been a sub-postmaster and, after much uncertainty and failure to get proper information out of the Post Office, he had resigned. It was a relief to be free from the long hours and a fifty-one-week year. He did not get the three months' notice he was entitled to; that he could put up with. But what had finally dished him was that the Post Office had come to life, after he had retired, with a decision to close the sub-post office. This left him with a small shop which, without its postal business, was very hard to sell. He had counted on a good price to provide for his retirement and now he could not count on a sale at any price. Meanwhile the business rates on the shop were ticking up as ever. Jammed between a pub and a fish shop he was in another kind of limbo, doomed not to have the 'nice little bungalow' which was his dream unless he could get another job and start saving for a deposit.

Relationship to work

All our informants in all four of our categories had recently come out of, or been pushed out of, paid jobs, and we have been considering what they had come into or been pushed into. What was now their relationship to their work? The broad division they made, and therefore made us make, was between unemployment – in which case they hoped to get back to work – and retirement – in which case they did not. Retirement was further subdivided in the manner we have described.

This division seemed to justify one of our basic decisions, to distinguish between a second age, which was the world of work to which people were committed because they had a job or wanted one, and the third age when this attachment had been given up. The unemployed were in the second age and the retired by and large in the third. The exceptional few amongst the retired (and the one medically retired) who had no wish whatever to give up work only illustrated in a different way the importance of the work/non-work criterion. These few could not be thought of as having the negative freedom of being disengaged from work whereas the others could. The upshot was that 36 people – all the 31 unemployed and 5 of the others – had to be regarded as still in the second age, the other 113 as in the third.

There is no doubt that the unemployed in the sample were the most hard done by in almost all ways. Their average age was certainly lower than the rest, but even that was a mixed blessing since their promised land of retirement was further away in the future. Their frustration was wanting work they had not been able to get. They paid a financial penalty too: most of them had nothing but the unemployment benefit, which was lower than the standard pension and many of the occupational pensions which others got even when there was no lump sum to go with them. They belonged to a large but neglected category of unfortunate people whose age had brought them disadvantage without compensatory advantage of any kind. They were at one extreme in a society which has been subject to increasing polarisation.

This showed up for other people in our sample, despite its being unrepresentative of the age group as a whole. There were the usual class differences between the people in our sample according to whether they were in the professional and managerial class, the clerical or the skilled, semi-skilled or unskilled manual. Sixteen of the thirty managerial and professional people had taken early retirement compared with eleven of the forty-eight semi-skilled and unskilled. Only three of the unemployed people were professionals or managers, the other twenty-seven of those in this social class being in one or other of the retirement categories. These three were therefore very much the exceptions and two of them had more resources to fall back on than almost any of the other unemployed. This did not mean that it was not a blow to lose their jobs. It is worth mentioning them because they are exceptions to the polarisation thesis and yet illustrate it all the same.

Mr Charles lost his director's job not because his company was closed down but because it was taken over for the third time in as many years. The first two take-overs he had survived. He had always given all he had to his employer, irrespective of what his job was, working an average of seventy hours a week, six days a week, all night if necessary. He continued to do so with the third company but it was not enough. The new company had a different style of doing business; he did not quite fit that style and so had to go. 'It was a blow, especially to my ego, when I thought I had a job for life.'

All the effort you put into it, then someone comes along and, bang, you're out. I'm not bitter about it – they paid me a good salary – but in retrospect you look back and say I could have done a lot less. With the old company I could have stayed on a consultancy basis but not with the new one.

At least his company did not go bankrupt, and he received two years' salary as compensation, with which he paid off the outstanding debt on his mortgage. He now enjoyed the boon of owning his own house mortgage-free. He, and all those like him, were in that way a good deal better off than the people – on the whole the poorer people anyway – who, as council tenants, had to go on paying rent as well as rates out of a much lower income, and those with mortgages still to keep up. It could be a struggle to maintain the mortgage payments even when they were rearranged and phased over a longer period. In the sample as a whole, only three of the thirty-six people who owned their homes outright had to change their pattern of spending significantly and make major economies, as compared with thirty-eight of the ninety council tenants.

Mr Jack was another director who went down with his company. He was worse off than Mr Charles. When it was forced into liquidation he was responsible for the other employees and had to sack them without necessarily having any rights to compensation of his own if the company's assets were not enough to pay the creditors in full; they were not. He had seen collapse coming, all the more sadly because the factory was full of machinery that they had put together recently, some of it in first-class condition: a new extension had been built a year or so previously, and there was still a good deal of work in hand. But faced with a cash-flow crisis, they had to close in a hurry. On the last day there was a creditors' meeting and afterwards Mr Jack called the workforce together and told them it was all over. 'There were a few mutterings but nothing more.' Then he walked around with the chief foreman to lock up, pondering what a terrible waste it all was with people wanting to work and the factory there fully equipped for them to work in. 'It was a bit grim. If ever we had to fight another war, God knows what would happen. We wouldn't have the men or the expertise.' Mr Jack himself had his house and some resources to fall back on so it was less of a disaster for him than it was for his company.

Mr Earle was the one who did not come out of it so well personally. He was more like the other unemployed. He had also been in management, in a firm doing asphalting. When it went into liquidation there was no money to pay him any occupational pension and he received only a small lump sum. Never having been unemployed before, he had no experience of what to do. Consequently, he did not sign on immediately and, when he did, he was sent to the wrong place for the forms he had to fill in and heard nothing for seven weeks. At the end of that period he was asked for pay-slips for the last two weeks of his employment and, since the firm no longer existed, these were not easy to come by. It took eleven weeks in all before he received any dole and twenty-one weeks before he received any housing benefit.

When he was at work Mr Earle earned up to £500 per week. At the time of the interview, about a year later, his income was down to less than £75. He was forced to make economies. Instead of baths, he washed down in the sink to save hot water. He did the laundry once a fortnight instead of once a week.

Partly so that he would be constantly aware of the small amount of electricity 50p would buy, he kept the coins in a special box by the slot meter; also, the light would not then go out for long, and the TV go off while he was groping around for the money. The problem he had not solved was drink. 'Drinks are the worry. I don't like to blag a pint, so I try to go in the pub when there won't be many people there so that I don't get a drink bought for me or have to buy drinks for anyone else.'

Social polarisation

Mr Earle reminds us again of the plight of so many of the informants who were at one extreme of a polarised distribution. Most of them did not have any cushion and, if they did, it was not a plump one. If they dropped out of the working world early, they forfeited many of the benefits of an occupational pension even if they had been in a firm which had one. As their savings were exhausted, they could sink even deeper into the underclass. Their disadvantages could continue to accumulate and at a faster rate. For many of them the handicap started at birth or not long after, with their health putting them under a lasting disadvantage. Healthier children have a better chance of succeeding at school and, later on, in the labour market. The handicap was liable to remain with them, just as the handicap of missing an apprenticeship had stayed with the Ford men.

For the population as a whole this kind of accumulated disadvantage has shown up most strikingly in comparative death rates. Mortality differentials between the social classes have widened continuously since 1951 and Wilkinson has related this not to the average incomes of different classes, because these have all gone up, but to the relative poverty of those at the bottom. 'Having drawn out the movements in relative poverty both before and after the early 1950s, the trends in mortality differentials which once appeared as an anomaly now seem more plausible.'*

* R.G. Wilkinson, 'Class Mortality Differentials, Income Distribution and Trends in Poverty 1921–1981'.

Another researcher has commented in similar vein.

> It now seems apparent that the post-World War II rise in
> relative social class mortality differentials is genuine and
> that additional research into its causes is warranted. This
> effort is made all the more imperative by the counter-intuit-
> ive nature of the results: social class inequality in mortality
> is shown to have been lowest during 1930–2 and 1949–53,
> by any criterion difficult periods for the national economy,
> and to have increased substantially as economic growth
> resumed during the late 1950s and 1960s. It is clear, then,
> that affluence alone cannot be relied upon to diminish dis-
> crepancies in the risk of premature death between socio-
> economic sub-groups of the population.*

Part of the explanation is that degenerative diseases – cancer
and heart disease – have become more important causes of death
and these are related to smoking, diet and exercise; and partly
that their work has been more wearing, more exhausting physi-
cally, more boring, done in more toxic environments. Mortality
is much higher for semi-skilled and unskilled workers than for
professionals, and the evidence for sickness is much the same.
For men generally, life expectancy at fifty has been rising only
very slowly since 1931, with a class bias to that too.

Proneness to unemployment is rather like proneness to disease.
It starts early and continues in an adult world which has become
increasingly competitive; those with less skills to offer get the
least good jobs and experience the highest turnover between
them. They have the worst pay and live in the worst housing.
And these cumulative disadvantages reach a peak at later ages.
When there is heavy unemployment it strikes with special force
against this age-group and, above all, against the marginal people
within it. Employees in steady jobs can stay in them and have a
chance of being promoted on grounds of seniority alone, so that
ageing can bring them an effortless affluence. They can enjoy
the accumulated benefits of unbroken seniority. If they do not

* E.R. Pamuk, 'Social Class Inequality in Mortality from 1921 to 1972 in
England and Wales'.

advance automatically year by year they often benefit from the internal labour market within their firms in which they get preference over outsiders for any vacancy that arises. When they retire they get an occupational pension in addition to their State pension. On the other hand, the unskilled manual workers, or people who were that before they were pushed out of work altogether, are usually pushed down as well as out. Unless this trend is checked, fewer of the most disadvantaged will struggle out of the second age in any state to enjoy the third. Fewer of them will benefit from the general increase in the expectation of life.

The one group can pass over or through the dangerous decades before the standard retirement age oblivious of the vulnerability of other people of the same age. As they ride in their cars on the elevated motorways they may hardly notice the people below. Those who have seldom had a steady job are automatically demoted because they have no seniority, being forced to put up with worse jobs in order to stay in work at all, or being pushed or drifting right out of the labour market, 'some skilled men taking labourers' jobs, some able-bodied labourers taking employment held normally in periods of lower unemployment by men with some disability or handicap'.* One lot of people go down the ladder while another are going up, one lot get worse off as another get better off.

There is nothing new in this kind of vulnerability to unemployment. As long ago as 1972, before the recession, another survey – as it happens made in Woolwich itself – showed that older workers took longer to find jobs once they were out of work,** and were more likely to drop out of the labour market altogether.

All our findings support the conclusion that for men the chief determinant of the costs of redundancy was age. The older workers were, the longer they took to find a job; the more likely it was to be a case of 'Hobson's choice'; the

* A. Sinfield, *The Long-term Unemployed*, p.50.
** McKay and Reid found that fifty-five was the threshold point beyond which people had particular difficulty in finding new work. See D.I. McKay and G.L. Reid, 'Redundancy, unemployment and manpower policy'.

more likely they were not to find a job at all; and the more likely the job was to be inferior to the one they had lost.*

They were also less fit and their general state of health was worse. Their disadvantages were even more pronounced three years later, and we are sure it would still be the same now.

Two people who had worked in the same industry can illustrate the polarity. Mr Travis had been the night manager for a newspaper distributor, for whom he had worked seven nights a week for thirty-two years. He had a stroke (ironically on one of his very few nights off) and was advised by the doctor not to return to work yet. On coming out of hospital he went back in order to return his set of keys to the safe. On hearing about his health the managing director stood up and said, 'I'm sorry to hear that', shook his hand and showed him out. A few weeks later an envelope arrived containing a cheque for the two weeks' holiday pay that he had accumulated. Nothing else, not even a compliments slip. No lump sum, no occupational pension, no contact.

Mr Traill was a journalist, latterly deputy foreign editor of a national newspaper by whom he had been employed for thirteen years. He inputted at midday what Mr Travis was responsible for distributing at midnight. As with many of our professionals he was self-made, having left school at fourteen. He had suffered the journalist's occupational disease: a heart attack following excessive smoking and drinking. Towards the end of his time he was working three or four days a week. The decision to leave was '60:40. They would have put up with my bad health, but I was getting a taxi to the office and it was becoming expensive.' An *ex gratia* payment of £10,000 on top of his lump sum, plus a pension of over £50 a week, softened any blow there was, by helping him indulge his passion for greyhounds. He was writing a book about them. His previous occupation left him with money and the skills with which to fill his time comfortably. His unseen and unknown distributor stayed in his deck-access flat in Thamesmead and, as it happened, he was quite unembittered.

* W.W. Daniel, 'Whatever happened to the workers in Woolwich?' p.119.

* * *

The people whom we have counted as in the second age could also be thought of as marginalised from both the second and the third age, in the Age Trap, condemned to try and return to the second age when there was little chance of succeeding. But if they could not get a job again, hundreds of thousands of them could at least be released into the third age; since the State is the principal gaoler there is a key.

The unemployed people had labelled themselves that partly because it was how others regarded them, and particularly because that is how they were regarded by the State. In the absence of any nod from others or any payment to them which would be more identifiable as a pension than a dole, indeed of anything which would show that they were old enough not to have to seek paid work any more, they had to remain in the negative condition, with the negative label of being without work, but without enjoying the crucial negative freedom of having detached themselves from the ordinary full-time work-force. They had not been released, and so could not release themselves, into a new age.

Retirement is a negative enough concept too, but since ageing is something that affects all of us, and is not so obviously attribu-table to any fault of ours (except where over-smoking, over-drinking or over-eating have advanced it), there can be no blame for it. If blame there be it should be nature's, and people as they get older do blame nature, roundly and repeatedly, as they notice each new sign of their age, their failing memory, their failing sight, their failing hearing, their failing appetite, their failing strength, their greying hair, their loss of recuperative power from illness, their liability to fall, and a hundred other slights that they have to blame something for if there is no someone to stand in for the something. At least they themselves are innocent. But in the labour market they are in a sense blamed for their age, particularly if they are working-class people without specialist skills. They age more rapidly, and die younger. They have had harder, tougher lives, as shown in their faces. Despite all that we said about age-averaging in Chapter 1, a working-class man at fifty can look as old as a middle-class one at seventy.

Employers make it worse by rubbing it in, while it is the fear that their powers are declining which makes so many of the Mr Trimmers and Mr Philpotts so desperate to demonstrate that they are not by any means as near to the grave as employers, who so cruelly remind them of it, seem to think they are.

The unemployed of this intermediary age are the victims of an injustice. They have been impaled by society on a dilemma: employers consider them too old for a job and the State too young for a pension. We shall return to the point in the final chapter. It is all a result of our conventional age-stratification and age-enumeration. People are assumed by the law of the State, but not by the practice of employers, to age at the same rate, as though they too are batches of machines whose common rates of obsolescence can be calculated with a fine and, in this case, devilish precision.

This need not be. State policy *could* greatly augment the third age population if State support were made payable at earlier ages. If this were done the number of medically retired might also go down. So many of them are in that category because they would be still worse off if they were counted as unemployed. Suggestibility being what it is, not only could fewer people be labelled as having a health problem but fewer people might actually have a health problem. Since health is one necessity for wellbeing, the gains could be impressive.

But most of our people were not unemployed but early or normally retired. They also were defined (but defined differently) in relation to the paid work they were no longer doing. If they were not working, what *were* they doing? This is the question we take up in the next chapter.

FOUR

The Restructuring of Time

'If every day is a do-as-you-like day you
don't have any good days.'
Mrs Bright, Eltham

The last two chapters have been about freedom from the hold
of full-time work which is the condition for entry to the third
age. We have argued that people can cross the threshold to a
different kind of life, even though they are doing paid work, as
long as it does not dominate; but they cannot if (like the domestic
staff at the British Hospital) they are still so attached to work
that they cannot make a new start. People full of regrets for a
past they have lost can hardly be ready for a future they might
be able to grasp. Nor can they if they are so hard pressed for
money or a respectable status that, on these grounds alone, they
hanker for an ordinary job. But once no longer tied to work, as
we judged 113 people in our sample not to be, they could be
regarded at any rate as third age candidates.

The critical division now is no longer between the second and
third age but, within the third age, between forms of freedom
which in the opening chapter we called the negative and the
positive. We have to be rather more precise about the distinction
than we were then in order to put people in one category or
another.

It was partly a matter of sheer activity; what people, in answer
to a number of our standard questions, said they 'did'. We went
over a long list of activities, asking them in various ways to tell
us what they had done and to fill out their own diary of how
they had spent their time. We could then add up the number of
events recorded in the diary, take account of the answers to
several questions about hobbies, sports or new interests they had
taken up, note their trips and holidays, and from all that get an
idea of how active different people were. Although there was a

bias towards physical activity because it is so much easier to ask questions about it, we bore in mind, of course, that 'mental activity' could be intense. Sitting quite still, a person could move from one poet and poem to another, one symphony to another, transport him or herself to the furthest limits of the universe, or traverse the history of science or the history of philately since stamps were first used. We did not regard Mrs Black as inactive because for several hours every day she retired to her own room to read the Bible or religious books or play religious tapes to herself; or because she spent so much time thinking about, and in her thoughts planning for, the little house she hoped to build for herself one day in her own Jamaican countryside. She intended to go back there after the last of her children had left her English home.

We did not regard her, or others like her, as in the negative category: it seemed indeed that mental and physical activity went together. Mr Player – 'I just creep about' – did not appear to have a rich mental life, whereas Mr Warburg, the Royal Gateman from the last chapter, made light of any disability he had when he talked about 'putting the world to rights' so far as lay within his power, by looking after the gardens of three neighbours older than himself, collecting stamps, making ship models and exhibiting regularly at the Royal Chrysanthemum Society which was all the more agreeable to him because of its Royal connection. His trembling fingers did not prevent him cultivating flowers.

Mr Thompson had also surmounted the disability brought about by the industrial injury he sustained as a roofer and aggravated by a stroke. Although he spent most of his time alone at home, he felt less bored and hemmed in than in his last job in a Remploy factory for disabled people. At 9.30 every morning he sat down to do the daily crossword before he began writing, either poetry or a science-fiction novel. One of his poems, on the Chernobyl disaster, had been read several times on Radio 4, and a love story about a disabled person had nearly been taken up for TV. He had organised local residents into a theatre group and he was writing a play for them. So although he said his health was 'much worse' than when he was working, he was less bored and less tired, and generally enjoyed life much more.

But it was not enough for our purpose to regard activity in

itself as the only necessary attribute of a candidate. We wanted to explore the relationship between the activities. Endlessly circling around a house with the vacuum cleaner, or going up and down to the corner shop, would not be enough. There had to be more of a pattern to what was done, and our special interest was in the patterning of time, or what we called time-structure.

We can focus on the nature of the challenge confronting retired people by considering again what they have left behind. All our informants except the virtually self-employed had moved from having their time controlled by others to having to control it themselves, at least to a larger extent than they had done before. Since one's time *is* oneself, employment by someone else cannot avoid being a partial slavery, albeit of a kind which most people (like the unemployed in the last chapter) are only too happy to seek out and submit to for the sake of the security, the rewards and the sense of mattering to others which it brings. If you do not want independence it can be a burden to have it thrust upon you. Emancipation was not always as popular with slaves as the emancipators believed it should be.

The control that work exercises over time is not just control over the time actually spent on it. Work dominates everything around it as a mountain dominates a plain. What comes before it each day is a preparation for it. Perhaps a man will take a quick look at his sweet peas if it is a fine day, or pull up a weed or two before he sets out. But most of what he does is getting ready for the work ahead, shaving and dressing himself so that he will be respectable when he gets there, eating so that he will be able to sustain himself until lunch, buying the petrol so that he will be able to deliver himself there on time, turning left or right where he always turns left or right. The employer's hand is on the wheel of the car. The evening is for recuperation. The weekend is also for resting and preparation, blocked in as it is between the end of one working week and the start of another. The same goes for the holidays allowed by the employer. So control of working time goes a long way towards being control of all time. People of the right age have to work or prepare for it or recuperate from it 7 days a week, 365 days a year.

Being without work is being without this organisational spine. Power over his or her time is handed over all at once to the individual. For forty-five years a person does what he or she is told, or expected to do, on the job and off the job, and suddenly, after a day much like the previous fifteen thousand days, the imperative is no more. Like it or not, chosen or not, the worker is an ex-worker, his or her own boss.

No longer is an employer going to decide what you do at 11 a.m. You are not self-employed, you are self-non-employed. You have to decide what to do with yourself. Even if you decide upon nothing, just to sail along in your chair, that too is a decision, even if by default. If you are not going to move into a state of autonomy you are exercising a choice. Fromm said that the individual in modern society remains unaware of powerlessness because it is 'covered over by the daily routine of his activities, by the assurance and approval he finds in his private or social relations, by success in business, by any number of distractions, by "having fun", "making contacts", "going places".'* Retirement removes some of the cover. But you may be only momentarily autonomous; you may bang the door shut as soon as a chink appears lest the light blind you.

Why is work so appealing?

Very few people from any occupation can manage the transition without some tremor. For some it is more like an earthquake. It is worth asking why this should be so. Why is work so appealing even when it is disliked? Why is it so difficult for people to escape from dependence upon what they have known, sufficiently to give a chance for any kind of positive liberty? It is partly our conditioning. In this (and almost every other) society it is drummed into us, even if less insistently than it was, that work is our vocation. If one follows Marie Jahoda one would say that, to offset the conditioning, it confers so many benefits: the pay, the social contacts, the status and sense of identity it gives, the feeling of being appreciated by someone else at least enough to make it worth their while to hand over money in the form of wages.

---

* E. Fromm, *The Fear of Freedom*, p.115.

There is also the sense of contributing something to other people beyond the workplace who are, as consumers, prepared to pay the employer or oneself for what one produces. Then there is the relief of being able to let someone else take the decisions instead of having to worry about them oneself. But if the tally were limited to that list, substantial as it is, a further major benefit of work would still be left out: the structure it gives to people's time.*

Time-structure cannot be literally visualised, like an object in space, but is no less important. A building, a human body or an organisation can be *seen* to have a structure. They are made up of various elements – bricks and steel, or floors and staircases; hearts, lungs and kidneys; personnel departments and accounts departments. These elements and their relationships constitute the structure. But partly because we have no organ for time as we have for sight, smell or hearing, it is harder to comprehend a structure in time which is not linked to a structure in space, as it is when an office is a day-space or a bedroom a night-space and a kitchen is for food. We are saying that the two main elements essential to a time-structure are routine and habit on the one hand and the opposite element, variety or contrast, on the other. But since they are not visible, the routine is to a large extent concealed and the contrast likewise. Like a building which has more of the principal floors under the ground than above it, the structure is hidden from view.

The concealment would be only superficial if people could readily accept that 'Man lives by drama, remembers by ritual and survives by routine'**; they could then also accept that they were slaves of routine, sleeping regularly in each twenty-four hours, getting up at more or less the same time on every weekday, eating meals at more or less regular intervals, regularly fulminating at the traffic, going through the same motions and perhaps emotions on any one workday as on another. But ordinarily they conceal these facts about themselves from themselves. In this game of solo played with themselves they usually win. Routines,

* M. Jahoda, *Employment and Unemployment – A Social Psychological Analysis*.
** John Morris, 'Three aspects of the person in social life', p.90.

merely by dint of being repeated day in, day out, or week in, week out, or year in, year out, or regularly with no such tie to a calendar, become embedded in habits and these are what give continuity to the structure. It is in the nature of habits that people do not recognise how strong their hold is, or even that they have them at all. We pick up a telephone when we hear a particular buzz, we pick up a fork when we see some food on our plate, we reach for the salt when we crack an egg, we pick up a pen or tap a keyboard when we want to leave a message, we pick up our language and our manner of speaking from listening to others. Being unaware of the habits we cannot be fully aware of the time-structure to which they belong.

Once a habit has been ground in we hardly know what we are doing or need to know. To know would be to remember how it all came about, and keeps coming about; mercifully, we can forget. It is not only totalitarian regimes which impose forgetting; we do it ourselves with an opposite effect, a liberating effect, but in a totalitarian manner. Thoreau says this of the path which led from his cabin in the woods to the nearby pond:

> It is remarkable how easily and insensibly we fall into a particular route, and make a beaten track for ourselves. I had not lived there a week before my feet wore a path from my door to the pond-side; and though it is five or six years since I trod it, it is still quite distinct . . . The surface of the earth is soft and impressible by the feet of men; and so with the paths which the mind travels.*

Any habit is a path. The first time one walks that way one may think about it a little, the second time one hardly does, and by the twentieth time it has become automatic. One merely follows in one's own footsteps. Other people coming that way do the same just as automatically, always building, within people and between people, on the same mimetic tendency. Any one of us can lay down a path which could last for a hundred or a

* H.D. Thoreau, *Walden* (Harmondsworth: Penguin, 1983), p.371. Ionescu (*Journal en miettes*) said likewise, 'Habit polishes time – you slip as you do on an overwaxed floor' (quoted by de Beauvoir, *Old Age*, p.376).

thousand years. Countless others will go on following it without knowing how it came about. Some of what has been is, and is what should be, world almost without end.

The repetitions are not just to be deplored. By coasting, relying on habits which have stood the test of experience (one's own or someone else's) to take us through one stock or standard situation after another, we can save time which would otherwise have to be spent on always thinking out afresh what has to be done. We can save our attention for what is not stock or standard but is in contrast with it and so fires our often latent alertness, and allows us to have and follow our own thoughts without necessarily being in silent collusion with others. A time-structure needs both elements, because people need both – regularity in the background and contrasts in the foreground. The regularity puts us into an automatic mode, the contrasts prick or jerk us out of it. Life has to be paragraphed.

The pattern is there in nature. All creatures (including us) respond to what chronobiologists call *Zeitgebers* – time-givers. The main ones come from astronomical movements which are as regular and as precisely regular as can be. Greenwich Mean Time has to keep time with them, that is with the daily revolution of the earth on its axis and the annual revolution of the earth around the sun. The monthly revolution of the moon around the earth is the third of the great *Zeitgebers*, in tune with the tides and hence the movements of many aquarian creatures as well as human menstrual cycles. The internal biological clocks of ourselves and all other animals which set the timing of all our internal bodily processes are synchronised with these astronomical clocks, the one that matters most being the daily one. The needs both for regularity and for contrast have their origin in these same astronomical movements, the point being that these are not only regular in themselves but, as there are three of them and their cycles are independent of each other, they also build a series of independent but interrelated contrasts into the environment. Creatures have to live with, and benefit from, the contrast between day and night and also the seasonal changes in temperature and in the length of day and night and the phases of the moon.

Even if they never went out of their houses, our informants

could not altogether avoid these primordial markers. But in an industrial society they have become much less important than they were, and are, for people who live in the open air or get their living from the soil or the sea. We have become less dependent on the sun and the moon, and more on a social universe which, although nested within the solar system, contains a partially separate system with its own timers. These have partially replaced the other *Zeitgebers* which cannot operate in an environment of artificial light and temperature in quite the way they did before. The new system of signalling is based on the mechanical clock, and all that is tied to the clock, with a great deal of assistance from routines. But not all people are equally affected by the social *Zeitgebers*; and if they do not have a paid job to confer a time structure they can be doubly deprived, of the contrasts and the regularities of both the natural and the social environment.

Routines can themselves be in contrast with each other. A short routine sequence which is repeated again and again and again with no break from it in the course of a day, and taking up most of it, can induce a painful boredom. There needs to be a half-way house between the strain of having too much variety and the boredom of having too little. There needs to be a break. No matter if it in turn leads into a routine as long as it is a different one, on a different frequency. The high frequency of repetition of the same routine within a working day is what is so wearing. But if routines on three-hourly or hourly or five-minute frequencies are a counterpoint to others which are daily, the outcome can be relatively harmonious.

It happens continuously. The repetitiveness of what is done many times over in the morning can be relieved by a lunch which comes but once a day, and the repetitiveness of lunch itself can be varied by eating different food on different days. If there is always fish on Fridays or beef on Sundays that too can be offset by more idiosyncratic regularities without necessarily switching around the time of lunch. In institutions it is usually at the same time each day. In music it would soon become boring if for long stretches the frequency of sounds remained as much the same, say, as the steady beating of one's own heart, with no variation in the number of beats in a bar. Composers of music and of the pattern of a day have to break free from the regularities they themselves create and find their own time outside their own time.

The pattern seems to be similar in both situations. A repetition of actions or notes or anything else builds up an expectation that there will be a further repetition of the same kind, and the more repetitions there are, the more firmly bedded becomes the expectation. The expectation arises out of one memory being superimposed upon another. But after a period the repetition ceases to be reassuring and becomes resented: we are bored; there is nothing to engage our attention; we ache for something different but it does not have to be so different that we cannot recognise it in its context. It is enough for there to be a change of key or tempo or for a daily or weekly or yearly or any other routine to cut across and bring to a temporary end the within-day routine.

Yesterday's lunch can be lodged in the memory long after it has passed through the stomach. But it is also partially wiped out. Routines are the less well-remembered the more they have been well-learned. It seems that the memory, not just of how to perform them but of a particular performance, can be partially wiped out by sleep. It has been suggested that the function of dreams, and therefore of the sleep in which dreams occur, is to clear the 'computer' of that day's memories and make familiars appear strangers. Each day can then seem much more a new day than it would otherwise be. Each night, like Penelope, we can unpick the tapestry we made yesterday but, unlike her with an Odysseus to wait for, without even knowing that we are doing it.

It follows from this that even the most humdrum day – unless the subject is in solitary confinement with only the same few feet for his same two feet to pace in – is lightened by some surprise. It need be only mock. In a piece of music one may have heard the sequence a hundred times and yet a particular change of key or tempo can still have the character of a surprise, though not a surprise at all, and, more surprising still, can be in some way more delightful the more times it has been repeated, so that it can be ever more fully anticipated and in a sense under control without taking the surprise away completely. So it is with the events of a working day. The mock-surprise of the knocking-off bell can seem not to be a mock-surprise at all. It can be as delicious (or more so) to confound a routine by a switch to another routine which derives from a different past without the special polish the present can give it as it would be if the break really represented a novelty. A complete novelty could be so much of a shock that it would freeze the young machinist and deprive him of the customary spring to his step as he hurries off for the umpteenth time to the company car-park after his day's work is done.

After the day's work is done – that is the point we have to stress. There is a sequence. There is an after as there is a before. The great advantage of work is that it is a contrast with non-work, and the two are in sequence so that this important contrast between them adds to, and sets off, all the other lesser contrasts within work and outside it. Each day, each week, each year and each lifetime displays this still central structural wall (particularly for men) which divides off what is done on one side of it from what is done on the other. We keep popping from one side to another and finding it a relief to do so. The work side may be dominant but there is still a sharp enough contrast to be worth savouring between work and what comes after.

Work is not considered work unless it is strenuous. At any rate in an industrial culture, if work is to be satisfactory it needs to be to some extent unsatisfactory: it needs to cause some fatigue in body or in mind. It needs to be persisted in for at least a little beyond what people 'want'. People need to continue with their routines, and make an effort to do so after some boredom or tiredness has set in. This is not so much because labour needs to be 'hard' if it is to relieve the conditioned guilt which was responsible for much of the hardship felt by the unemployed people we featured in the last chapter; it is more because the relaxation brought on by the counterposing of another routine can then be more complete because the contrast is greater. For most people work without effort is not work that will create leisure. There is no leisure if there is only leisure. But where there is tension there can be relaxation, and that kind of tension can have as important a function for people after retirement as it did before.

Expecting the relief is itself a relief. Time can be moving at two different paces simultaneously. As it draws near, every worker can be looking forward to 'knocking-off time'. The mild discomfort of doing something so difficult that it becomes tiring, or of doing it for so long that it becomes monotonous, can be softened, perhaps even softened away, by anticipation. People can look forward to enjoying a relief which they have earned by having to continue an activity beyond the point where it comes easily to continue it. To postpone pleasure at all requires a discipline which can be bearable if it pops up its own reward.

The change from one routine to another is more of a relief, when it happens and in anticipation, if the time at which the change occurs is itself routine. There needs to be a scaffolding of regularity. Its purpose is more fully achieved if it happens each day at around about five (or at some other regular time) than if it happens sometimes at two and sometimes at six in an erratic manner. One can deplore the precision which marks turning points in the life cycle, and treats all people as though they are ageing at just the same rate, however old they are, and still see the attraction of a series of turning points occurring at more or less the same time during a series of days, weeks or years. Without this kind of temporal regularity there could be no industrial society: people would not catch the trains or arrive at work or have hot meals together because no one would know when to cook them. But some regularity is not just other-imposed, and self-imposed, as a necessity of the whole industrial order; it is also a necessity as much of internal psychic order as of external social order.

What has all this got to do with positive liberty? If there are regularities and breakaways from regularity which can also, to some extent, be regularised, we could regard them as yet another set of impediments to people's liberty. Freedom from a time-structure could be regarded (and has sometimes been regarded) as one of the basic freedoms. But that is not our premise. In our view, unless time has a structure of some such kind as we have been describing, people can all too easily be overcome by it. Time can become the enemy in more ways than one. Without a good deal of regularity in their lives, the power to act can be taken away from people. We give some examples later in this chapter. Most people cannot manage without a structure. This does not mean they cannot enjoy positive liberty but that they can only have it if there is some 'order' in their lives. They can then use that order as a platform on which to build their own liberties. The standard contrasts can set off and stimulate spontaneous contrasts. People can appreciate moments and movements in their own heart and head which belong only to a moment which transcends, as it were escapes from, its necessary foundation in the regular, the known, the unsurprising, the reassuring. From the standard compost can spring a flower unique in its fragile beauty.

If the contrasts matter as much as we have been suggesting, one would expect the moments when there is a switch from one routine to another, or from any regular sequence into one which is not routine at all, to be moments when people are most vividly aware of the passage of time, and yet escape from it into a kind of eternity, and feel perhaps most poignantly alive. The transitions are often marked, as they were by the people in our survey, by some kind of *rite de passage*, all the way from small rituals which underline the significance of almost trivial changes to those which do the same for major ones. There can be a tiny ritual when a woman takes her own cup from the special place where she keeps it to be filled up when the tea-trolley comes round, or when a man hides in the gents for a cigarette with one of his mates. People change their tone of voice as they say goodnight to each other when they are leaving their offices or factories before the good night has come. Like a *Cutty Sark* or another tea-clipper racing for Nanking with her topsails filling with wind, they can emphasise what a substantial venture it is that engages them by hurrying every day to the station to catch the 5.35 train home with the absorbed, far-away look of serious people who cannot brook delay until they relax at the end of *that* routine into the next one as a train-commuter. If they do not make the transition by collective transport they can enjoy the illusion of being alone in their own mobile decompression chamber where they can both day-dream and simultaneously compete frenetically, not as sleep-walkers but as sleep-drivers. At night when they arrive at their second workplace and step through its front door, if they have not already changed and left their working clothes in a locker, they can change from their one-kind-of-working boots or shoes into their other-kind-of-working slippers before they put the kettle on and get their tools out.

Some of the rituals to which people particularly drew our attention were those which mark retirement. We were constantly surprised by how crucial they were when they did not happen. For example, Mr Court had no grouse about his financial settlement – a lump sum of £32,000 – when he was compulsorily retired by the Co-operative Store of which he had been manager. But before that, despite a take-over, he had thought he was safe until retirement. A month previously he had even been offered a new car. Then suddenly he was told he was sacked. It knocked the stuffing out of him.

> At retirement you get a framed certificate, lunch with your wife and a long-service award. I've been done out of all that. The men at one depot took me out for a meal and gave me a presentation but another depot never gave me even a card. I was invited to someone else's 'do' but I just put the phone down. I feel kicked out, forgotten. It gets your goat. I feel unwanted. I've done forty-four years with the firm and I would have had forty-seven years service when I'd eventually retired.

Mr Duke was a postman who had also been deprived of any proper ceremony.

> I was disappointed. I went in for the early retirement scheme and nothing was confirmed so I took a fortnight's leave. I was to resume duty on the Monday and then I got a letter from Runcorn telling me I was retiring the next day. It was a bum's rush. I simply went up and saw my friends and had a drink.

Another manager employed by a local council had been forced into early retirement by his unduly high blood pressure. But he still hoped that his long service would be recognised.

> I took wine in and some eats. I was presented with a camera from the staff. There was nobody there from the council.

That was it. Full stop. I left at 2 p.m. Later, after I had been away for some weeks, I was called back and given the 'Shield of Bromley' for long service. It was a case of 'Oh, I'll give you this, Joe'.

Mr Trimble, an electroplater, had been forced into retirement one year early. But it was enough to spoil it for him. 'I missed the presentation at sixty-five.' He had been looking forward to it for years. Mr Jolliffe's leaving was flawed in a different way. He had worked for thirty-seven years for a foundry, becoming towards the end a stamper of bronze as well as a checker. On his last day he was given a cheque for £89 by his immediate friends at work, then taken along to the boardroom, where his superiors and a director presented him with another cheque, for £370, and a bronze bowl. It was insulting, Mr Jolliffe felt, that his bowl had a fault, a 'blow-hole', a bubble of air which marred the smooth surface – considering that he had been a checker-stamper whose job it had been to reject shoddy work!

To outsiders like us the leaving ceremonies, when they did take place, were not very elaborate. But this did not stop them from mattering greatly to the people they were for. The transition from work to non-working life called for a major adjustment. It was as much of a turning point as other key transitions in life, like leaving school or college or the single status, all the more so because it might not be clear what people would do once they left. The least enviable state at this critical point, to judge by the evidence of the last chapter, was to remain on the labour market but without a job. The most enviable state was to be normally retired after a small ritual that was loaded with some special significance, and not on the labour market. There could be a good deal of confusing ambiguity about which it was unless it was made clear to people how they could now regard themselves.

Some, as we have seen, tried to be judges in their own cause and label themselves 'early retired' in order to remove the ambiguity. But this was less satisfactory than having the status endorsed by others, especially one's employer. The employer could show, on behalf of society, that one was entitled to retire by reason of all the good service one had rendered, and in this could act as proxy for a whole chain of previous employers. Fair financial treatment was indicative that one had earned it. So, in a symbolic fashion, could be the manner in which the departure was recognised. There needed to be some display of feeling. When there was none, nor even any gathering to mark the occasion, something was missing. A ceremony could be convincingly comforting, as it was for Mr Follett, a factory handyman who had a party at the works with drinks all round. He then took his work-mates to the club for two hours and was presented with three symbolic gifts related to his hobbies, a cut-glass ashtray, a walking stick and a dictionary, as well as a card signed by everyone. Mr Spear, too, was grateful to his trade union for insisting that his leaving should be treated in a 'dignified' way. 'A party was laid on by the company with drinks, cheques were given over and the directors *had* to be present.' A question we shall take up again in the last chapter is whether there is any way in which the departure from work could be marked for the generality of people.

The two kinds of third age

We now come back to the consideration of whether people are going to be categorised as either negative or positive in our special senses, not just according to their level of activity, but according to whether their activities had the kind of structure of regularities syncopated by contrasts that we have been describing. The two criteria overlap. If someone engages in many activities they will ordinarily have some routines and contrasts between them, and so qualify for the active category on both counts. But this was not always the case. A person could have many activities so similar to each other that contrast was lacking, and without that there could be no structure. Which category anyone fell into could not be wholly cut-and-dried, with weighted scores on different questions being assembled into a composite index. We asked a series of questions about the events people used to mark the passage from day to evening; whether different parts of the day passed quickly or slowly; how if at all they differentiated between weekdays and weekend; and what differences the seasons made to them. But we also had to consider the general impression people made. We had, in other words, to use our own discretion in comparing one person with another, especially when judging one person to have a relatively differentiated time-structure and another not. Discretion introduces an arbitrary element into the analysis; but not to have used it, to have confined ourselves entirely to questions which could have a quantitative answer, would have been even more open to error.

There was no problem about the categorisation of people who were at the extremes. It was sometimes almost enough to compare their diaries; for example, Mr Savoy's, a busy local councillor, and Mr Sawyer's, who was not busy at all.

We will come back to Mr Sawyer. For his part Mr Savoy was obviously active but, more than this, he had an array of markers in his day. He is an example of a positive third ager who was, in effect, continuing to work, although in an occupation for which he was not paid. He did not 'go' to work in the same way he had before. But the same familiar markers were there because, although he did not leave the house and return to it at the same hours he had before, his wife and daughter were both in paid jobs and did so. His day between their departures and returns was punctuated by his 'Council work', as he referred to it, and he further differentiated his time with some selective TV watching and a crossword puzzle, to which he returned when there was a gap. Asked to name some events in the day which he found memorable, he chose his leisurely breakfast, his wife's return from work, and the evening council meeting. Like Mr Sawyer, he 'would be lost without clocks'. But his problem was not to space out the day's emptiness so much as to cope with its fullness. He said of the mornings, 'My God, that's gone quickly, and I haven't done all the things I wanted to do.' Late at night, after a busy day, he did not like to go to bed, because 'there's always too much to do'. What he meant was that he needed a period of relaxation when he could let go and luxuriate in a flow of time when markers could be dispensed with. He was busy enough to have leisure. He relished the contrast between the more and the less strenuous, the periods when time seemed to go faster and slower. According to our approach, Mr Savoy was

Mr Savoy's Diary		Mr Sawyer's Diary	
12 p.m.	Reading		
1.15	Went to bed		
6.45	Awakened by teasmade	6.30	Woke up
7.00	Tea in bed with wife	7.00	TV
7.15	Lay talking with wife, as she prepares to leave for work	7.15	3 cups of tea
8.00	Wife left, got up		
8.15	Washed, dressed		
8.30	Went for paper		
8.45	Put kettle on	9.15	TV off
9.00	Breakfast and read paper	9.30	Hoover and housework
10.00	Phone call from wife		
10.15	Phone call from daughter		
10.30	Rang housing office, discussed case		
11.15	Typed couple of letters	11.30	Sandwich
11.45	Went to post them		
12.00	Had neighbour come about a problem		
12.15	Rang office re case etc.	12.30	Tele news
1.00	Looked at crossword puzzle	1.00	Walk to social club
1.15	Wife rang	1.15	Pool and darts
1.30	Prepared and ate light lunch		
2.00	Washed up, tidied up		
2.30	Watched snooker on TV		
3.00	Put casserole on low gas		
3.30	Went to visit lady re problem	3.45	Get home
4.00	Went to mobile library		
4.15	Had cuppa	4.15	Sleep
4.30	Finish crossword puzzle		
5.00	Pages to read for council meeting		
5.45	Washed ready for meal	5.30	Wake up
6.15	Had dinner (wife and daughter home)	6.00	News, tele all evening
7.00	Attending council meeting		
10.30	Rang wife, she collected me		
11.00	Supper and watched sport on TV		
12.00	Wife went to bed – I watched on		

a positive third ager with some money and an occupation, even if unpaid, which he could easily substitute for his paid one.

Others were like him in continuing to hold and enlarge

interests related to their job. Mr Oates of Thamesmead was one. In his last years as a mining engineer he had allowed his hobbies to take up more of the time paid for by the employer by way of wage rather than by way of occupational pension. He may even have 'retired' before his formal retirement. His new/old life was shown by the extent to which he was a kind of freelance organiser. He helped to manage a number of professional institutions. Bland and extrovert, he was no doubt as happy as he used to be at the evening meetings of engineers, greeted by and greeting a wide range of people by their first names. He also dealt with his correspondence after breakfast when he was not talking to people he called 'workmen' – this just as he presumably did when he still had a work-office as well as a home-office. Then on two days in the afternoon, after a siesta on the sofa, he settled down for several hours to one of his hobbies, either pinning butterflies – he was a lepidopterist – or preparing some of his slides for another of his celebrated slide shows. On Saturdays he went to collectors' markets looking for butterflies just as he had done for many years before.

Mr Sutcliffe's church was his work. He was a provincial grand knight of the Knights of St Columba. On a typical weekday he would officiate for a funeral and follow that by a talk with the church architect arranging for a repair to be done in the church office. The day before he had been so busy he had not been able to get down to work on the church account books and had had to bring them home in the evening, just as if he were still in an ordinary job which would not stay contained within ordinary working hours. There was no let up at weekends. Sundays were absorbed by the bell-ringing that he also organised. Another of our informants, Mr Crane, was a toolmaker who had prepared for retirement by setting up a fully equipped metal workshop in his back kitchen. He was also an elder in the United Reform Church and it looked as though he was going to bring his interests together by making metal objects for the church. He showed us some metal candle snuffers he had just finished.

Mr Penny had a different kind of occupation which his job, before he happily gave it up, had interfered with. He 'retired' from one to settle into another. He could only spare a short time each morning for a walk before he took out his form books and picked the horses he thought would have a good chance that day. A comparison of the odds from the bookmaker with the ones he arrived at by his own calculation enabled him to decide whether to bet or not. If he decided to, he went down to the betting office to place his bets or placed late ones over the telephone and then watched the afternoon's races on the TV. He also had a share in the ownership of a racehorse and went to see it whenever it was running. He was a single-interest man and an absorbed one, but even so with a good deal of contrast within his day apart from the basic one between the winners and the losers in the races which were either winners or losers for him. Mr Roger was like Mr Penny except that his passion was greyhounds rather than horses. He had bought some pedigree dogs and was breeding, training and racing them assiduously.

Mr Castle had been a section engineer at a brewery which had treated him generously when he asked for early retirement – two lump sums of £10,000 each and a weekly pension of £50. He spent part of his time back at the brewery where he took visiting parties on tours for which he was also well paid. He had another part-time 'job' working on a city farm. He had also continued with his 'traditional' pursuits such as bowls and golf but was trying not to overdo them lest he become addicted. He was planning to spend some money on going abroad for a few weeks each winter and taking shorter trips in between.

Mr Howard's new job was the study of genealogy. Instead of going to his job as a Telecom engineering instructor, he went off most days to the Public Record Office where he had acquired a regular's ticket.

Some others who had been office workers had now taken up manual work. Several said how much they enjoyed it – revelled was one of the words used – as an ex-police inspector was now 'revelling' in marquetry. Miss Hamble had been the head of department in a large pharmaceutical company, having gained a biochemistry qualification by evening study and day release. Now that she was retired she liked having the chance to get to know the neighbours. For the first time it seemed like a 'village atmos-

phere'. She liked above all to work with her hands, as she had
learned to do at woodwork and tailoring classes. Mr Morrison
had recently married and regretted that his wife was still working
full-time. 'I dread her going to work because I'm left on my own.
I'm all right once she's actually left – it's just her going. It's
just the loneliness of it.' But it was at least some compensation
that after long years at a desk – he had been an administrator
in the NHS – everything he did was manual work. In this he
included golf, swimming, cycling, caravanning, fishing – all
'manual tasks'. Yet others had launched themselves on new
hobbies, or consolidated old, by taking evening classes in oil
painting, in pottery, in dancing.

Many people like these were not just active third agers, they
were highly active, and the question must be raised about them –
were they like this partly because if 'old' at all they were definitely the young old? We chose the sample the way we did partly
because we wanted people who were not yet old but would
become so. That is one way of quizzing the future.

But when they were older would they still be as active? We
thought we might be able to catch a glimpse of how things might
turn out by looking at some of the people who were in their
early or middle sixties, and had 'slowed down', such as Mr
Durham and Miss Prendergast. Mr Durham had been for the
previous thirty-five years a self-employed greengrocer and a very
busy one, working sixty hours a week, fifty-two weeks a year.
The job was important to him financially and for the place it
gave him in the community. He was content with the hours he
worked and found that time passed very quickly. Bank Holidays
were his only time off. He looked forward to the pub at
lunchtimes and also found a lot of interest in his shop in talking
to people – 'everyone's different'. But after thinking about it for
nearly a year he was also glad to give it up when he reached
sixty-four – it was entirely his own decision. The last day
was a normal working day – 'Met customers, many expressed
regret that we were leaving'. When retirement came it was 'a
blessing' – the first day felt 'Fantastic – I felt free to please myself
how I spent the day'. He loved his 'free time', got used to it
immediately, and said that he saw life as 'one long holiday'. He
still looked forward to a pint in the pub at dinner-time as before.

Otherwise he attended to his two hobbies, the two folk arts of Britain, DIY and gardening, but considered himself 'too old' to start evening classes. Despite being much less busy than before, he said time passed more quickly because he was enjoying it. 'I never consider the clock; a job takes as long as it takes.' He and his wife's joint income had dropped a good deal but was still adequate and they had not found it necessary to cut down their spending at all drastically. Mr Durham had not felt the need to substitute a hectic round of new activities for the old: he was happy to savour his days, do less and 'take his time' over it.

Miss Prendergast was medically retired. But like Mr Savoy she was determined to make the most of her life after work, even if it meant a continual compromise with her illness. She lived alone, very independent, and dreaded becoming 'a burden' when she could no longer manage by herself. She loved the job she had held for ten years in the personnel department of ICI. It was full of variety and she was proud to have been part of it. She had had many opportunities to travel and made close friends that way. But her attitude to *working* rather than the job itself had changed over the last four years as she became increasingly afflicted with arthritis. This limited her – she had to spend one of the weekend days resting, couldn't always leave for work on time because she would wake up very stiff and she found it a physical relief to get out of the office at lunchtimes. Health rather than work became her preoccupation as she became worn down and tired by her disability. She 'felt dishonest' about not being able to cope fully with the job. She was given the opportunity of continuing to work part-time but decided against it, mainly for financial reasons. She would not have been able to draw invalidity benefit and a mobility allowance. As it was, she retired on a pension of £5,000 p.a. and received a lump sum of £15,000 with which she improved her house and took a holiday, besides keeping some in reserve as savings. She also supplemented her income by letting a flat in her house. It hadn't proved necessary to cut down her spending, except on clothes. She felt that money 'impinges on everything' but not too much on her. She was evidently a careful manager.

Immediately after giving up work she felt 'a bit flat', partly from tiredness. The leisurely pace at which she now lived was 'so mixed up with this arthritis – it halves what you can do'. But even so she filled her time with varied activities, some of them new for her– gardening, cooking and writing as well as painting – and was more active now in the evenings because she was less tired. She never got bored and had taught herself to appreciate being at home, whereas in years past she was hardly ever there. She still travelled, though not as far afield as she used to. Since retirement she had been to Germany three times, and at the time of the interview she intended going there at least once again. Her greatest man friend was a German.

Miss Prendergast was visited again a couple of years later. Although she had originally thought of moving from her house to a stairless flat as her arthritis progressed, she had by then abandoned the idea. Instead, she had withdrawn more and more from the upper parts of the house to the small basement flat. She now rarely had to climb the stairs. Money helped her again. The basement had a kitchen and no bathroom but she was able to install a downstairs cloakroom. The basement was at the same level as her conservatory and her beautifully-kept garden. 'Never' at home in her years as a single working woman, she now felt her life was so centred on her house, her garden, and the upstairs lodgers who were also her friends, that she could hardly bear to leave it, and certainly would no longer consider moving house. She could afford to pay for cleaning and gardening. A car from Motability financed by the State mobility allowance was also a boon; it meant that despite her disability she could still get to the local shops and visit her sister half an hour's drive away.

The trips to Germany had continued though she was not sure how long they could go on. Despite the attentiveness of airport staff, she found the fuss over cars and wheelchairs increasingly trying. Being so much in the public eye, especially alone in the crowds, was also embarrassing. 'You feel like a crab scuttling along to the departure lounge.' Her increasing handicap was still a serious worry – though it had been overtaken by the diagnosis of a more serious illness. A recent operation had revealed an inoperable cancer. Though shocked and bewildered at first, Miss Prendergast seemed to have come to terms even with this new misfortune. She almost welcomed the prospect of a rather short fatal illness instead of a slow and painful decline.

Pace of time

Miss Prendergast is one of those people we classify as positive third agers: she not only had relatively high levels of activity, she also had a time-structure made up of routines and contrasts, of routines that had the effortful character of work and others that did not. An incidental benefit of having such a time structure shows itself in the pace at which time seems to pass. The objective is caught up in the subjective. If there are no contrasts, or few, time can seem to go slowly, even painfully so. This is not just singly but doubly unfortunate, because time which goes very slowly in the present to the point of extreme boredom can seem to go very fast when it is past. As recalled in memory, if it can be recalled at all, time can go as fast as a racing car or a speeding aeroplane which becomes only a blur. This happens when there is nothing to remember a passage of time by, no markers, no contrasts. So people with very little to hang on to in the present are twice handicapped – time goes both too slowly for comfort in the present and too fast for comfort as recalled.

The opposite is the state which people (who have not been demoralised) strive for, where the present seems to go briskly but not so fast as to make everything into another kind of blur (one is as it were *in* the racing car rather than watching it); and where in retrospect, according to this rule of opposites, the past-present seems to have gone relatively slowly, where, in William James's words, 'a time filled with varied and interesting experience seems short in passing, but long as we look back'.* The past can then become a resource in the present and a means of constructing a future because there is so much to dwell on that was interesting enough to record in the memory. The ideal rhythm, in the constant juxtaposing of past and present which makes up so much of our mental activity, is not slow-fast (which is so difficult to manage in dancing) but fast-slow, that is fairly

* W. James, *The Principles of Psychology* (New York: Dover, 1950), Vol.1, p.624.

fast in the present and fairly slow in the past as it is recalled. This seems to be the proper tempo for the third age, as it was enjoyed by some of our informants, and a good way of adding yet another contrast between the past and the present to the structure of time.

What we have been saying so far about the pace at which time passes can apply to people generally. People can lose their time-structure at any age although it is, no doubt, more common to do so when they leave paid work behind them. But we are claiming that it is particularly necessary for older people to maintain a structure because time seems anyway to go faster than it did earlier in their lives. This is due to nothing else except their age; it is a very common experience that time speeds up as people get older. We suggest that this is in good part due to two factors over which people have some but not very much control. The first is that, within a time structure, the contrasts become less sharp the more they are repeats of what has happened before. In childhood when contrast – say between winter and summer or between the cold of an outdoors and the warmth of an indoors or an ordinary day and a birthday or Christmas Day – is being experienced for one of the first occasions, it can be wonderfully vivid. In old age it has all happened so often before that the freshness can have gone. Some of this freshness can be preserved by cultivating new experiences even in the later years; difficult as it may be to find the new when so much has already been experienced, it is never too late.

The second factor is the way in which memory fades from the time in life when it was at its most retentive (and learning consequently quickest). But the loss is not all loss by any means. Long-term memory can be affected hardly at all: people's memories of their childhood can become more rather than less vivid as they get older. Short-term memory is what suffers. William James wrote of the intuited past which belongs to the very short-term memory. This intuited past is continually rolling along in the present, even if it forms a distinctive just-past part of the present, 'the rearward portion of the present space of time',*

* W. James, p.643.

which does not have to be recalled by any kind of conscious effort any more than sights have to be perceived through the eyes by making a conscious effort. James contrasted the intuited past with the conceived past which is stored in memory – 'the knowledge of a former state of mind after it has already dropped from consciousness'. According to this terminology we are saying that the sharpness of the intuited past is more eroded by age than the conceived.

Common observation bears this out. People get more 'absent-minded' as they get older; in other words, they are more liable to forget what they have just been doing or intended to do, leaving the toothpaste off the toothbrush without meaning to or finding themselves with a telephone receiver in their hand wondering whom they were going to ring. The intuited past can have many gaps in it or, as one might put it, less of the intuited past is stored for even a short period in a form in which it can be recalled. If that is so, then there is less of the immediate past to remember and time can seem to run rather than just pass. If all time-markers were forgotten then there would be no sense whatsoever of time passing because there would be nothing by which to measure the speed of its passage, just as a person with a blindfold would not be readily able to gauge the speed of a car whose suspension was so good it did not vibrate as speed increased. But some markers remain intact – a year, a day, the intervals between meals or between the clock announcing the hours – and yet between the markers less of the intuited past has become embedded, however insecurely, in the conceived past. If this is so, then time will best be slowed down by deliberately training one's memory, even though there may well be a physiological change in operation as well as everything else. Memory is like all other faculties in being liable to atrophy with disuse. The more the faculty is exercised at any age, the better condition it will be in and the more of a brake be kept on the tendency of time to gallop.

As far as memory goes, our active third agers had taken one step to preserve it by finding a rhythm made up of contrasts and markers so that there was at least something to remember when they were thrown on their own devices. But we cannot pretend that in this respect they had found a quite new way of life. They mostly 'kept busy' and so kept time from slowing down too much. The happy mean would be a different balance between fast and slow in the present which would also be a different balance between fast and slow in memory. Perhaps, once the third age is more firmly established than it is now, there will be some new ways of moving towards the period when people become less outwardly active. Sorokin,* one of the few sociologists who has written extensively about time, pleaded for a treatment of it which takes account of the subjective and so does not 'bleach' time of its essence. The cultivation of unbleached time could be matter for a new kind of demography of the subjective which would show how subjective longevity could be increased without robbing the present of its immediacy. In subjective terms people may all eventually be able to be double centenarians if that is what they want.

The negative third agers

Our examples so far have been of the positive; now it is the turn of the negative. None of our people was like Nelson Mandela in being for long stretches in solitary confinement when, as he is reported as saying, 'You came face to face with time and there is nothing more terrifying than to be alone with sheer time'.** But none of our people were in an ordinary prison and, however passive, they could not avoid some of the routines and contrasts of ordinary life. After their sleep most of our people started their days in the way they had always done. Getting out of bed in the morning was followed by the same sequences as of old – a cup of tea, washing, dressing, getting breakfast, preparing for what the new day would bring even though it brought nothing new apart from itself and they could not say, with Thoreau, 'Only that day dawns to which we are awake. There is more day to dawn. The sun is but a morning star.'*** But at least the new day was something of a beginning. The let-down could come

* P. Sorokin, *Sociocultural Causality, Space and Time*, Ch.4.
** F. Meer, *Higher Than Hope* (Harmondsworth: Penguin, 1990), p.268.
*** Thoreau, *Walden*, p.382.

later when the person who was not going to work had to listen to all the other people in the street (whom he recognised more by their cars than by themselves) as one by one they shut their front doors behind them and started up the engines of their 'mobile rooms' until there was again a silence not unlike that of night. In that disquieting quiet Mr Soloman waited for the postman to come up his garden path and the plop as the junk mail which he carefully wrote off for dropped reassuringly to his floor.

After the day had fairly begun the problems could also begin of how to pass the time and maintain a structure, painfully contrived as it could seem. Mr Hastings' was organised around his household cleaning. The work was precious; it was impossible to pretend there was much more of it than in fact there was. To an outsider the house was spotless enough not to need attention for weeks. But each day he managed to spin it out so that he would never finish 'too soon'. 'I have the fear of my whole routine going. So it's reassuring to look at my watch and know that I've got things done by a certain time and not let things slip.' 'I try not to let things slip' was said often, as though there was an abyss into which 'things' might literally slip unless a big effort was made. Like T.S. Eliot's Mr Prufrock measuring out his life in coffee-spoons, Mr Sawyer measured out his in teaspoons, cigarettes and treacle-sandwiches. 'I have a fag every two hours to make the time pass. It's the same with cups of tea and at 11.30 every morning I treat myself to a treacle sandwich.'

Evening could bring some relief: people could then join in the working rhythm by proxy, as Mr Cannon did with the customary aid of the clock. He used to come home at five to start his 'evening'. Now at five-ish he did just the same, stopping whatever he had been doing and relaxing. 'I feel that I'm on my own time.' Mr English at five likewise stopped whatever he was doing and changed his clothes and started something else. The television with its on-the-dot programming could make the evenings the same as they had always been. Mr Rayne: 'The evening begins when the wife hoovers all round the TV.' They were, from that transition onwards, focused on *the* centre of the room and ready for the news at 6 p.m. and an evening's spotlessly clean viewing. Sometimes it was the news, sometimes the daily instalment of a familiar soap opera unfolding itself like the days themselves. 'The evening starts with *Emmerdale Farm*.' Or sometimes it was when the local pub opened at five-thirty.

For others, pets set the time-structure: not just a living creature to appreciate, even to love, and to be appreciated and apparently even loved by, but also a time-keeper to order one's day by. Dogs and cats get easily locked into external *Zeitgebers*. They are, to use another term from chronobiology, 'entrained' by markers created in the first place by their owners. The markers become second nature for the animals themselves, and then at one remove for their owners. They can both enjoy a congenial mutual imprisonment. Dogs that are exercised at the same time twice a day, stir themselves from their sleep at the appointed hour, wag their tails, look up beseechingly at their owners and put their paws on the back of the chair to demand their regular walk. Knowing that a dog would tell the time, Mrs Clough bought one to drag her husband out of the house regularly. There was a happy realisation that the time had come – 'Oh, my goodness, is it that time already?' – before experiencing the mild boredom induced by traversing the same street day after day with sniffing dog not quite at heel. It never seemed to bore the dog. Mr Crowe was as strangely pleased when at 4 p.m. precisely every day the fish in his aquarium came to the surface to be fed. They were as regular as any TV News in signalling the beginning of the end of another long afternoon. After he had given his fish theirs, Mr Crowe allowed himself a little treat. The fish gave him his cup of tea.

The week

The end of the week was another marker that hardly anyone could avoid. The week is entirely man-made, without any tie to astronomy, and the weekend is a construct of 'work', consisting of the days when it is suspended. Its value comes from the contrast between weekdays which are also working days and weekend days which are not. That will still be true if the 'weekend' gradually puffs itself out to encompass first Friday afternoon and then Friday morning (as happened formerly with Saturdays) without necessarily shortening the number of hours worked in the week. As it becomes shorter, the working week could become even more precious than the weekend.

A few people were irritated by the weekend just because there was so little differentiation from the week. Mr Neill's weekend had invaded and absorbed his week. 'Every day is a Sunday without the bloody church bells.' But most still took some pleasure in it. Some *were* church-goers. They did go out to the pub on a Saturday night, they did watch the sport on TV on Saturdays. They did see the children whom they could not see in the week. Mr Trimmer collected all his children in a van every Saturday and spent as much of the day as he could with them. 'Saturday is always family day', he said. 'If it's a nice day we take a run down to the coast.' Or they postponed the shopping until Saturday. Mr Clipper still preferred weekends to weekdays not because he relaxed then but because he didn't. There were more people around, more bustle, he could join the other cars in the queue for the shopping car-park. After that he could again, as in old times, join the great society which was queueing up at the checkout, whereas if he and his wife shopped on a weekday the absence of others would make them conspicuous by their presence and they could be made to feel they 'ought' to be at work. On Saturdays he was no more under that pressure than the young couples with their restless children.

Mr Uphall and his wife managed to keep weekends as weekends by preserving the small ritual that had always initiated them. On Friday nights they bought in a few cans of beer and had a scratch meal, not because he did not have time to prepare the same supper he got on other weekdays for his wife, who was still working, as because the scratchness of the meal marked for him and for her the difference between the week and the weekend. The demarcation was further maintained on the Saturday morning. Whilst Mrs Uphall shopped at Sainsbury's her husband did the hoovering at home, again just as he used to. He had all week to do the hoovering, and the shopping too for that matter, but they both preferred to go on as they had always gone on.

For many of the people like Mr and Mrs Uphall, who had not been overcome by losing their week, it was not so bad by any means. They had had a hard life of toil or distress and they continued something like their customary daily, weekly and annual routines without complaint. They had not been ambitious either about their working lives or what was to come after. They did not expect anything more of retirement than that it would be a relief from the grind of work. This was a real enough relief for the many who had not enjoyed their work even while they were grateful for the money it brought. This has, very broadly, been the working-class experience well beyond the Ford factory. If that was their background, the negative form of the third age could be a happy enough contrast with the demanding working life which preceded it.

Time structure collapses

So with the aid of their markers, and some inventiveness, most people we classified as negative third agers succeeded in getting by, and often enjoying it. But a few did not. They were not unlike the men of Marienthal with their 'empty time', though none of them spoke of it in that way. The standard cliché, as if time was not Father Time but a kind of deadweight jellyfish pulling them down and preventing them from doing anything, was that 'time hangs heavy on my hands' – again the hint of a big drop below. We have thought of them as having a 'collapsed' time structure with even less activity and fewer contrasts than the people like Mr Hastings we mentioned earlier. There were sixteen of these, and they were all men. None of the women in our sample suffered in this way. We have included amongst the sixteen, six people who were counted as in the second age because they were unemployed or waiting to find work. They are brought back here because as far as time-structure was concerned the second agers, being somewhat like the men of Marienthal, were in this respect indistinguishable from the third agers. If second agers are excluded we were left with ten third agers who were not only passive but passive enough to be considered as being at the extreme.

Another characteristic of these people was that besides being men they were manual workers. As such they had not been used to any (or not much) autonomy while they were still at work. In our sample as a whole only one in five of the unskilled or semi-skilled manual workers had had the chance when at work to decide for themselves how much time they gave to one task or another, compared with three out of five of the managers and professionals. Of the former, four out of five had to clock on or sign on at work compared with one in three of the latter. The jobs of these manual workers had not prepared them for the autonomy that was now thrust on them.

The common characteristic of the sixteen men was that their time was so undifferentiated that they now had a struggle to maintain even a minimal structure. If this was chaos it had something of the character of a void. Mr Player may have found it particularly difficult to adjust to being without work because his job had a notably fixed routine. He had been a milkman and 'I could say exactly where I'd be to the minute on the milkround'. It had been so tiring that he had no energy for doing anything else when not at work except recuperate from it. When he got home he was, like a soldier after battle, liable to fall asleep with one boot on and one boot off and a cup of tea going cold by the side of his chair. Now that he was no longer so busy or so tired it was in a way still worse. 'Time is all the same to me now. Last Sunday I could have sworn it was Monday. Every day is the same.'

Mr Philpott was like some much older people who have uncoupled the sharpest difference in everyday life – between sleeping and working – from the counterpart contrast between night and day. They can then doze through the day. Mr Philpott had not gone quite as far as that. He did not go to bed till four in the morning, often after having watched videos. His main sleep was in the afternoon. Then, after drinking three bottles of Guinness as a soporific, he would go to bed. Mr Groom did have a routine but with almost no contrasts in it, unless the contrasts in the fantasy life he led through his obsession with soap operas (handsomely fed every day) counted as such. Despite or because of the obsession he felt extremely bored. 'It seems as if I'm sitting here waiting for the end to come, doing nothing.' He could watch the TV in the middle of the night as well as by day by using his video. Video enables people to detach themselves from the ordinary daily cycle and its *Zeitgebers*.

He could not imagine any future for himself apart from a continuation of this dreariness, which might become more so. His one companion, his dog, was dying. He had thought about the future only as far as to decide he would not get another lest it might eventually be as bereft as himself. A new dog would probably die after he did and then what would happen to the dog when the dog was alone?

Almost all were putting up a struggle. Mr Sawyer, whose diary was displayed earlier, was doing so with some success. 'My body gets me up in the morning; I tried to stay in bed later, but I couldn't.' Having got up, he waited 'for the morning to go by'. The 12.30 news on TV was the crucial point in the day, a kind of axis on which it turned. He waited for it greedily, but would not switch the telly on until exactly 12.30. He then got shaved and dressed, walked to the club (but not before exactly 1 p.m.) and then spent the afternoon playing pool with some other men. Time, which had dragged obstinately all morning, suddenly accelerated and went 'too quickly'; but on his return he had to have a sleep 'to pass the time' until he could turn on the 6 p.m. news to usher in the evening. Some of the third agers like Mr Sawyer must be the best informed people in the country about the news of each day, the hectic activity of the world taking the place of the no-news of their own day and days. He deliberately moved from one stepping-stone in the day to another, from one news broadcast to another. Distinguishing between the days was another problem; he missed his birthday and only found out about it when someone reminded him. Every second Sunday one son took him home to dinner, and some afternoons another son took him out for lunch and to another social club for the afternoon. Without these weekly events, his sense of time beyond that of the day could have dissolved completely. Beyond the week there was nothing. 'I've cancelled all my (insurance) policies and told my son, let the council bury me. Everything's cancelled.'

Mr West was in a similar plight. For him Sundays were more or less the same as the days of the week. 'The mornings – I get so browned off and bored. It's only the dogs that get me up. If it wasn't for them I'd still be in bed now.' He sometimes wondered whether to give up. 'My grandad committed suicide. He was about my age and couldn't get work because of his age. I feel just like him at times.'*

Mr Aziz seemed to have withdrawn even more fully. He did nothing in the house but just sat for most of the day, listless and at a loss. He did not want to know what the time was. The only clock in his room was one and a half hours slow. He was even more extreme than most of the people in Marienthal. He did not even go out of the house to pace up and down the street or 'loaf'. Since immigrating a decade ago from Pakistan he had had a number of jobs, the last being on the Thames barrage. His wife and grown-up daughter worked full-time on night shift in a rubber factory. There were other children in the house but they looked after themselves. Mr Aziz' only recorded activity was to make himself a cup of tea, and then only if he was on his own. He was an example of one for whom negative liberty really did seem a tragic gift. When such people could no longer rely on the time structure that had been imposed on them during their working lives, they were unable to create one for themselves. Whereas once they had been imposd upon by slave-drivers now they were their own slave-sleepers.

* * *

The examples in this chapter have been of third agers who were either positive or negative. How many were there of each? The division was an arbitrary one, especially in the middle where the two categories got close to overlapping. But we made the decision as best we could and the outcome was that, out of the 113 people in the third age, 73 were put in the negative category along with Mr Hastings and Mr Aziz; and of them 10 were at the extreme. This left 40 in the other category along with Mr Durham and Miss Prendergast. The negatives out-numbered the

---

* 'Research has also examined parasuicide ("attempted suicide" or "deliberate self-harm") as a function of unemployment. Individual level studies again reveal a particularly high probability of parasuicide among the unemployed, especially among those without a job for more than a year.' P. Warr, *Work, Unemployment and Mental Health*, p.205.

positives by about two to one. If the proportions in the country as a whole are at all like this, there is a long way to go before anyone can be satisfied with the present condition of the third age.

But of more interest than the breakdown in the numbers is what has emerged about the character of the third age, and particularly about the activities of retired people and their time patterns. Some possess a clearly differentiated time-structure, the others do not.

The polarisation of the last chapter has reappeared in a different form in this. Some people were unable to create a new time structure for themselves when they no longer had paid work to do it for them. They had had a hard life before and in a different way it got harder when they retired. They were mostly manual workers and the disadvantages from which they had suffered before reached a culmination after retirement. The work that had structured (or over-structured) their lives had also so incapacitated some of them that they could not take advantage of their new freedom, showing that a satisfactory third age needs to be prepared for in the second and the first. When some of these people were thrown back on their own resources, they had none.

Others had been able to use their freedom to good effect. They had more variety in their lives than when they had been at work. There were also many similarities between the effortful unpaid work they had now taken up and the effortful paid work they had given up, or which had given them up. Some of them belonged to the 'informal economy'.

> The informal economy is important to our analysis of the future of work because it is the residual economy; it is the place where society's unused demand for work ends up. It is the reservoir of work. Reservoirs may look like pools of idle water, but they are recognised to be the right way to channel and conserve an excess of supply.*

The kind of work that positive third agers did had the great advantage that it had been chosen by them: it was what they

---

* C.B. Handy, *The Future of Work*, p.42.

wanted to do. Not many people at any age had such a range of choice about their work as these people who no longer had to do it. The third age was for some of them the age of a new freedom.

The distinction between negative and positive liberty does not now have quite the same aspect as it did when we first introduced it. The fortunate third agers used their freedom in order to limit it, and this was in accord with the supposition stated earlier. They employed their positive liberty in order to limit their negative liberty by placing constraints upon themselves. Their routines were constraints that they chose to impose. The unfortunates who did not impose such constraints upon themselves ended up having no positive liberty at all.

Structure is evidently necessary if people are to lead full lives, a structure that does not have to be imposed, as it is upon second agers. Structure can be chosen and, once it is, and the conditions for positive freedom met, people can flourish exceedingly.

FIVE

Cables and Cats' Cradles: Convergence between Men and Women

'I don't get much free time. I do all the
housework and cooking and look after my
grandson – that passes the time away.'
Mr Stephens, Kidbrooke

We would like to characterise the difference between the sexes by two images. For men time has traditionally been more like a huge single span, a central cable whose core has been his full-time continuous work; wound around, to be sure, with regular short periods of leisure chopped up to match the daily, weekly and annual rounds; wound around with the great events of family life, the births, the marriages and the deaths; wound around with unemployment; but nevertheless a continuous single strand running high above individual events all the way from adolescence to senescence.

Women have had to knit together different strands, especially their two sorts of work, whose rewards may be monetary or more fundamental than that, into a more complex whole. The pattern can be likened not so much to a cable as a swaying cat's cradle of twists and turns and overlaps. The elements of time-structure are the same as we described them in the last chapter: the routines and the contrasts between them, the variations between the routines and the changes of pace. But the part played by measurement is different. Variable task-time matters more in the home than standard clock-time. With clock-time in its pure form a person works or performs any other act for a standardised number of minutes or hours and then stops, as happened to an almost surrealist degree in the Ford factory. It is not like that when the task itself determines how long it takes and how long it takes varies from one occasion to another. You cannot pin down a baby to feed for the same number of minutes every day. The clock may be hanging hopefully on the kitchen wall but many tasks cannot be squeezed into standard daily slots; the tasks have to be woven together rather than assembled as in a factory. Also, instead of the contrasts being strung out in a linear fashion they have become more nearly simultaneous. There may be no leisure to follow work – that may be a male construct, not really apt for people whose work is never done – or, if there is leisure, it may come in smaller blocks so mixed up with work that the distinction may seem hardly worth making as long as the work that is done is, for all its repetitiveness, done in the home under the control of the self-employed 'worker' whose workplace it is.*

If this is as true about women as we think it is – the metaphors of cables and cradles seem to us to be quite apt – it follows that women are better prepared for the third age than men are. Men have customarily had more of a commitment to paid work, even if they have not been able to get it, and because of that they can be lost when they no longer have what has been central to their lives. Women, even if in this respect they are moving closer to men, have not moved all the way by any means. Their experience in weaving together different strands, their experience in coping with transitions between different statuses, their experience in shaping their identities from a variety of models rather than so much from one – are all conducive to making the best of a way of life after retirement that does not differ so much from their lives before. Partly because of this, partly because they have been *the* carers in society, women's personalities may well be less brittle, more elastic, than men's. If one strand in the cat's cradle is snipped, the rest can hold together without unravelling, the cradle subtly adjusting itself to take up the slack.

Not that this particular kind of cradle ever makes for an easy life. Organising time along the line of the cable can be a relatively simple affair. All that has to be done is to leave work when others do so and go home when they do. But someone with a

* K. Davies, *Women and Time: Weaving the Strands of Everyday Life*, p.37.

job and children has to be continuously aware of where the children have to be at any time and make arrangements for them as well as herself. If she works in a factory she has to keep school-time as well as factory-time.* Scheduling it all can be an intricate business as these two examples illustrate.

For tightness of scheduling the Black family was hard to beat. Mrs Black lived with her daughter, a single parent who worked as a nurse on the night-shift – this because no other working arrangement would be as much of a dovetail. They shared responsibility for the granddaughter who was at school. Each morning, after getting the granddaughter ready, the older Mrs Black waited at her door until she saw her daughter's car – as indispensable to the split-minute timing as if it too had been a person, making the trio of care into a quartet – swing into one end of the street. She then, without waiting to say good morning or good night, set off as fast as she could walk in the other direction to be sure of catching her train to her work, leaving the child on her own only for the minute it took her daughter to reverse into a parking place.

Mrs Cream was the knitter-together of even more strands. Mr Cream had worked seven nights a week for over twenty years, clocking up (as they say) massive amounts of overtime and the money which enabled him to buy a house large enough for himself as the manager of the home, their six children, a cousin and his mother-in-law. His wife had to ensure that he could sleep off his nightly labours, keeping the children occupied and quiet, whether they were at home or whether in the summer they went off for the day to the coast. If he went with them he would park himself in a deck-chair on the beach and sleep for the day while she supervised the children, threatening 'to knock their blocks off' if they woke him up. She too had a job, at the time of our first interview with her, as a bus attendant taking handicapped children to and from school. This was a split-shift operation which allowed her to spend most of the day at home with her sleeping husband. In this she had the assistance not of a car but of two motorbikes which snuggled together under a green tarpaulin when neither of the bikes was on duty. In the

* See T.K. Hareven, *Family Time and Industrial Time.*

morning she rode motorbike no.1 down to the garage where she left it and boarded the bus in which the children went to their special school. At the school she picked up motorbike no.2 and rode it home, reversing the sequence for the journey to and from school in the afternoon.

Towards symmetry

Mrs Black and Mrs Cream had a more cat's cradle-like structure to their lives than either of their husbands. This is because they had paid as well as onerous unpaid jobs. The notion of the third age is less apt for them. Nor would it be so appropriate for women who do no paid work at all or even for many others who work only until they marry and have children. The first group of women might never qualify for the third age because they would never have entered the second. The second group would have entered the third age when they were twenty-three or twenty-eight or whenever they withdrew from the labour force to devote themselves to their other labours in the home. The third age would have had a very odd constitution if it contained a host of young women and few old men.

But the notion does now have some relevance for women as well as men, and has been made more so by one of the most striking social changes of the century, the convergence between the sexes, most notably in the labour market. There have been many ways of describing the shift but for our purposes we are going to follow the description in *The Symmetrical Family*,* of which Michael Young was the co-author nearly twenty years ago. It proposed that the modern family was symmetrical in a manner which it had not been for several centuries since the family as the unit of domestic production was first overtaken by the Industrial Revolution. The husband who had been almost an alien to his family when he was working long hours at exhausting jobs and sharing his leisure with other men in pub, club and football ground had returned to the home to sit in front of the telly with his own wife and children. As fertility fell and with it the size of families, wives were less taken up with their

* M. Young and P. Willmott, *The Symmetrical Family*.

responsibilities to their extended families and wider kinship groups and were, like their husbands, more focused on their own immediate families, their children and also their spouses. More significantly still, the roles of the sexes had become less segregated and begun to converge, the increasing engagement of women in the labour force being one crucial factor and feminism another: as a result, more women had taken to work outside the home and men to doing more of it inside. Both men and women were shifting not to complete equality – far from it – but to a relationship which contrasted both opposition and similarity; and that great 'continental drift' in the relationship between the sexes has continued to wind its way through, and modify, the social structure. We shall in this chapter discuss each of the main trends as they have affected people of the same ages as in our sample – the move of women into paid work and the move of men into unpaid work in the home – starting with the first of them.

The convergence between men and women in the labour market has taken four main forms:

1 Men have done less paid work in the course of their lives and women no less. Figures from the Technical Change Centre showed that men's hours have dropped from an estimated lifetime total of 118,000 for those finishing paid work in 1951 to 88,000 for those finishing in 1981.* The figure for women remained exactly constant, at 40,000. Men still work on average more hours per week for more weeks per year, but the gap has been closing.

2 The reduction in men's hours has not been so much in the length of working weeks or years but in the length of working life. It did not show up so much in the middle years or in the weekly hours for men still in jobs. The vast majority of men between twenty and fifty have still worked continuously and continuously full-time. It is after fifty that there has been most convergence, with the number of men in the labour force falling, the number of women rising.

* P. Armstrong, *Technical Change and Reductions in Life Hours of Work*, pp.27–8.

3 More men have had to change jobs as they got older, and (especially in manual work) often enough take ones that, even though full-time, are inferior to those they had before. The downward movement of the men brought more of them into the same kind of jobs that were once considered women's jobs and into part-time jobs.* Many older men have experienced a degree of marginalisation.

4 The most decisive change is that the position of men in the labour market, at any rate working-class men, has become more ambiguous and so in that respect more like that of women. Not very many of the people in our sample could describe themselves with full certainty – unemployed and wanting or seeking work, unemployed and having given up trying to get it, or retired according to one of the meanings of that word. Our people were all without work. But even if they had had it, it did not follow they knew what occupation they could call theirs. They might have had so many different ones. If you have been a butcher, baker and candlestick-maker in short order, which of them is you?

The uncertainty is something that many women have had to get used to, even try to relish. If you leave a job to have a child, are you still a worker with other work to do? Are you intending to return as soon as you can? When will that be? And what kind of job will you go for? In-and-outness is inevitable, and even tolerable, when the needs of a family have to be juggled with those of a job, and on both sides the needs are constantly changing. The divisions have not been clear-cut and after mid-life it has been becoming more like that for men too.

For many men the changes have *not* been welcome. The driving force has been the labour market as it has become more and more competitive. In many low-paid and low-status occupations, especially ones not much shaped by technology in which labour costs are a high proportion of total costs, employers have turned to those with the least clout whom they could pick up cheaply

* See Angela Dale and Claire Bamford, 'Older Workers and the Peripheral Workforce: The Erosion of Gender Differences'.

and sack without compunction. The losers have been the new proletariat, the underclass subject to the polarisation referred to before. It consists of some young people of both sexes, women of almost all ages, and older men. So far they have had no Ben Tillett or Annie Besant to lead them, no modern general workers' unions to organise their disparate groups into a coalition of the underprivileged. They have a common economic interest that has not been converted into an interest group.

Disagreeable as some of the changes have been, they have led to more women being employed than in the past. The further consequence is that more women have had to retire in the same sort of way as men. On this account they are as much candidates for the third age as men. To illustrate, we will take two women who retired after holding down straightforward jobs of the kind that could as well have been filled by men. One was thrown by retirement but was making a recovery, while the other had welcomed it from the start.

Mrs Ash was exceptional in a number of ways. She had had an uninterrupted career, except for a short spell of maternity leave following a miscarriage. To her regret she had never had any children – she found the hardest time of day for her, now that she had no job to go to, was between 3.30 and 5.30 when she could hear other people's children coming home.* Time and time again we noticed that ears rather than their other senses made people aware of neighbours. Their sounds were their presence.

Mrs Ash had been employed by the Central Electricity Generating Board. When its Deptford generating plant was closed she was offered a job at another power station that was much too far away. She had always expected she would be at work at least until the proper age of sixty, and probably later still. So it was perhaps not surprising that she should be shocked. On the first day of having no work to go to she did have to sign on. She hit

---

* In a different context – the study of bereavement – widows reported 'attacks of breathlessness and "choking sensations" at the time of day when the spouse – the husband in all instances – had formerly returned from work'. C.M. Parkes and R.S. Weiss, *Recovery from Bereavement* (New York: Basic Books, 1983), p.15.

another car on her way home from the Department of Employment. 'I just reversed into it. I was not of this world. I came home and sat staring at myself the whole day. And it carried on like that till we went off to Spain for our holiday.' Like several other people in our sample under a similar stress she took to drink: she drank too much because she had too little to do. She pulled out of it by starting her own business as a reflexologist, massaging the feet and the other problems of her clients. But she was still mildly bereaved, pining for her proper work.

Mrs Bright was the other. She had a man's cable in her life but without a man's attachment to it. She had three children and was still astonished that since her divorce she had succeeded in bringing them up herself, always without the kind of job which would have made it easy.

My ambition was to be a public lavatory cleaner. The kids would have known where to come and find me and I could have sat there all day reading – Life of Reilly really. I could have studied as well, not to get a better job, understand me, but English Literature. No Maths – I only like numbers when they've got a £ sign in front of them.

She would have liked to have bettered herself in that way. Otherwise she had been well enough satisfied with the job she had had for many years as a cleaner not of lavatories but of offices. She had no other ambition. 'I'm an oddball. I want to keep my brains for my hobbies. If I had to use my brains for work that would take all the pleasure out of it.' The kind of job which would have used her brains would also have distracted her from her children.

But her cleaning job had once given up on her and she went to the Labour Exchange to see if they could help her. They couldn't.

I went down the Labour Exchange and was shitting and shotting the civil servants there. They were so stupid I couldn't believe it. I went round saying this so people said all right why don't you do it? So I was hoist on my own petard.

She took the clerical grade exam for British Telecom, passed and had stayed in it ever since. She did not become a creature of the bureaucracy but bent it a little for the sake of her family. She got up at 5.30 a.m. to be there by 6.45, an hour and a quarter before the office opened. As a result she felt she could breeze out early in the evening, and did. She got through most of her work, checking engineers' time sheets ('most of which were like *War and Peace*, not a word was true') in the first part of the day starting early as she did, and then relaxing in the afternoon, in this like the Ford workers. The work was so humdrum it would have been like breathing if it had not been for the change of pace. Her afternoon wind-down was not popular in the office any more than it had been in the factory. 'My guv'nor tried to get me to do more once but I threw a wobbly.' Outside her work her life was even more closely tied into an absolute routine. 'It's got to be, hasn't it? I raised the three kids, so it was one to the nursery at this time, two to the school at that time and so on. You simply could not deviate.'

When the children were young she earned £4.10s of which 16s went on rent and 25s on nursery fees. She was refused a grant for school uniforms for her children although she was a good deal poorer than others who were getting it. This made her 'spiteful' towards all public officials. She had only once in her life had enough money for a holiday.

> When I had a yard and a half of kids I thought 'when you're old enough you won't see your mum's arse for dust'. But you learn to live with yourself. When they were grown up I was talked into going to the Isle of Wight. The moment I got there I was counting the days. I couldn't wait to get back to dirty Waterloo.

Her current satisfaction came from a sense that she'd served her time – forty-four working years – and partly from the sheer novelty of being paid to do nothing. Her money dropping regularly through the letterbox was a source of wonder. Time was not a tragic gift but a glorious one. She was almost as glad to have no children at home as to have no paid work. Leaving work was 'like being in the delivery room and you've just delivered –

my God it's a relief. Then it was the beginning of another traumatic life but with this there's no catch to it.' And about the children –

Everyone said 'you'll break down when they go'. But I couldn't wait to get rid of them. I had three 'glads'. 'I'll be glad when you're five and go to school; I'll be glad when you go to work; and I'll be glad when you get married and out of the house.' I said to them 'You'd better have hateful kids so you know what I've been through.'

'They've gone a bit toffee. They've all got their wheels outside and hands dripping with gold.' She saw them hardly at all but got on with her grandchildren and spent a good deal of time with them. The rhythm with them was in happy contrast with what it was like with her own children.

With my children everything was a rush but I've got time with the grandchildren. When they're here nothing gets done, only the cooking, because we've got better things to do, playing silly games and having a song.

She knew she needed contrasts. 'If every day was a do-as-you-like day you don't have any good days.' So she made her own structure. She had met an old lady in a sheltered housing scheme nearby and she went up to 'sit with her for four hours on three afternoons a week, and talked and talked'. At nights and on one or two other days she had the free time she never had while she still had a job. Her evening began about 7.30 after she'd had dinner, washed up, hand-washed her clothes, had a bath and got into her nightie. 'Then that's my free time. What's on the box? Not a lot. On the radio? Not a lot. Right, get out your book.' Mrs Bright had plenty of contrasts within her day and week but the one which mattered most to her (as to several other relatively contented people) was between the relentlessly busy life she used to lead when she was at the 'beck and call' of others and the more relaxed days she was now able to enjoy. It was as though on each relatively peaceful day in the present she was able to compare it with the past by conjuring up from her memory one or more of those other days when it had all been go-go and tick-tock. She was as much a third ager as any man, and an active one, even more so than Mrs Ash.

Convergence after retirement

So where have we got to? There has been one kind of convergence between the sexes in relation to employment. Fewer older men are in work and more older women, and their experience of retirement is not necessarily so different. But after retirement has there been any similar convergence in the family?

The question can be underlined by bringing out again the point about the Marienthal study which we first made in Chapter 1.

Time in Marienthal has a dual nature; it is different for men and women. For the men, the division of days into hours has long since lost all meaning. Getting up, the midday meal, going to bed, are the only remaining points of reference. In between, time elapses without anyone really knowing what has taken place ... For the women the day is filled with work. They cook and scrub, stitch, take care of the children, fret over the accounts, and are allowed little leisure by the housework that becomes, if anything, more difficult at a time when resources shrink ... (Women) are merely unpaid, not really unemployed. They have the household to run, which fully occupies their day. Their work has a definite purpose, with numerous fixed tasks, functions and duties that make for regularity ... Watching the women at their work, it is hard to believe that they used to do all this on top of an 8-hour day in the factory.*

According to our view of the symmetrical family that kind of segregation of roles should be quite different now. Was it in practice amongst our people?

We said earlier on that the entry of women into paid employ-

---

* M. Jahoda et al, *Marienthal*, p.67, p.76.

ment has itself altered the domestic roles of both sexes. When there are two breadwinners the husband is under greater pressure to take on some of the responsibilities of the home. But it does not necessarily happen: it does not follow that because the wife becomes a husband, the husband becomes a wife.

In some households where the wives were also housewives the atmosphere was such that we almost expected to (but did not) hear them complaining that now their husbands were retired the husbands were, in the old phrase, 'getting under their feet' as they tried to get on with the essential work of the home. But Mr English said he had to go out and walk around so that his wife could do the chores without being upset by his being there. 'I get in the way a bit.' Mr Briar was the same. Mrs Briar could not do what she had to do if he was there. 'She had a routine. I mucked it up. She used to say "Don't forget to go out on Tuesdays and Thursdays".' In the Forest family avoiding housework was apparently more his disinclination than hers. Mr Forest annoyed his wife by just sitting around. She would round on him, saying 'Can't you make yourself useful?', and he would reply that he'd never done any housework and didn't intend to, and that despite having been a building worker he was never a DIY man and never would be. He also told us how content he was. 'There's never a dull moment.'

But it was more common for domestic roles to be shared. On shopping, for example, the men in our sample spent as much time on it as the women whose preserve it had once been, nearly an hour and a half a day on average. There was less equality in other spheres. Domestic work took men three hours a day on average as compared with four and a half for women. Some of that, though we do not know exactly how much, was the routine cleaning and cooking and so forth that ordinarily makes up domestic work. But the words used to describe such activities by the men were not always what they seemed. Mr Dickinson, when questioned about his previous day, announced proudly that he had cooked the dinner which was a far cry from the shamefacedness there would once have been about doing 'woman's work'. But on further questioning it seemed that his pride did not have all that much justification. It had been a stew, but what sort of stew? What went into it he did not know. His wife had bought and prepared the ingredients. All he had done was put the dish on to the top rack of the oven and turned on the gas. Even if such exaggeration had been taken at its face value, husbands did less domestic work of an ordinary routine sort, and more of the irregular (but, for the retired especially, not all that irregular) jobs around the house on the repairs, decoration and maintenance which are almost as essential for the house as for the man. As the men did less on domestic work, they had more time for what is sometimes called 'passive leisure': watching TV, listening to the radio, reading and talking. On this there was a reversal of what happened with domestic work, husbands spending almost four and a half hours a day on it and wives not quite three hours. But differences notwithstanding, they cannot be counted as substantial.

Some men had been pretty well compelled to become house-husbands because they were retired or unemployed and their wives were still working. There were twenty-six such men. Mr Urwin (the Royal Marine from Chapter 3) was one of them. He retained his self-respect by paying his wife housekeeping money as he had always done while he was still at work. He had never asked her how much she earned any more than she had asked him. He found the money for her by drawing down his savings to top up his disability benefit. But his savings were soon to run out. What was he to do then? He already felt like a kept man. When she eventually retired there would be another problem too: she would get a lump sum and a pension that he would not yet be eligible for.

Mr Schreiner was more usual in accepting his new station in life. He had been a manager of a hostel for down-and-outs who lost his job when the hostel was amalgamated with another. As his wife still worked, he had taken over a lot of the household tasks, regularly getting dinner and tea for both of them. Mr Wheeler always got up first to make his wife a cup of tea. He drove her to work and was waiting outside her office in the evening like a chauffeur. The evening used to start as he left the factory – now it started when he left her office. Mr Roger had a structure to his day which also revolved around his wife. He got up early to take her to work and brought her home at night to the dinner he had already prepared. Mr Cain said: 'I look forward to the evening because my wife is there – evenings begin when I hear her footsteps outside'. He stayed home in winter but went out with her more often in the summer. Mr Austen and Mr Spear were much the same. Their days, and their weeks, were structured as tightly by their wives' work as they had once been by their own.

Then there were a number of couples who had retired simultaneously. Mrs Neill, for instance, took early retirement when her husband was taken sick and they both moved to Greenwich to live with her daughter – a reminder that our sample was by no means composed only of long-term Greenwich residents. Mr and Mrs Dobson were both ill and gave up their shop altogether. Mr Archer gave up work because of his illness and his wife did so at the same time – it was not worthwhile for her to stay on as her earnings would have reduced the State benefit for her husband pound for pound. Several other people also explained this was why they retired together. Mrs Wilson had retired early herself and her husband thought it made sense to do the same. He said: 'We've got on better since I stopped. We're closer; the travelling to work kept us apart.'

Mr and Mrs Younger had seen very little of each other for many years because of his long hours on shiftwork. When she had a stroke he continued to work but he worried more and more about his wife 'being stuck in the house all day' and he gave up his job a full year before his official retirement in order to keep her company. There were no children, just the two of them, and now they spent all their time together. Mr Younger's 'activity level' was low. His shiftwork had so severely constricted their social life that they only had one friend which hardly made up for not having any children. 'Only one person thinks of us. He's a cousin who takes us for a day to his house once a year. It's the only time the wife gets out of the house except in the summer.' But the activity he had chosen was being with his wife and looking after her and he was intent on making up for all the years when they had seen so little of each other.

Mrs Salmon was in the same situation, retiring to care for her husband. He was very much the centre of her life (after years of working long and unusual hours as a waitress, which she loved), and she says she and her husband 'pace themselves' without reference to the clock. This meant she took things at an easier pace than she had – her husband's pace. She also got up during each night to help him to the lavatory. She'd taken up new activities since retirement – knitting and some child-minding – but they were chosen because they did not interfere with her care of her husband. Both Mr Younger and Mrs Salmon thought of themselves as fully occupied. Marriage to a partner who had become disabled dominated their lives, and they had both accepted this without feeling trapped by it.

Mr Welsh retired from being a clerical officer at a Co-operative Store at the compulsory age of sixty-five. His wife had prepared him for it. 'She broke me in gently, and when I'd got it settled in my mind I looked forward to it.' If his wife was not his right-hand she was, as he put it, his 'left-hand'. 'The main thing is your partner. We've been very close all our lives. We're happiest when we're together.' Since he'd been at home she had begun every day by asking him 'What do you want to do today?' The answer was usually the same. On consecutive days they did the household work together, went shopping together, worked in the garden together, and then settled down together for the same evening activity as the great majority of the others living on the meridian.

The alternate generations

Where people like those in our sample were fortunate enough to have children and their children children, the third age was bound up not only with the second age but the first. The relationship between the third age and the first is itself a measure of how far grandfathers (as another index of symmetry) are engaged along with grandmothers. Anthropologists refer to the principle of the 'merging of the alternate generations'. The merger is not brought about by the exercise of authority. The grandparents do not have to keep their grandchildren in order, nor the grandchildren obey. They can, with a warmth not offset by the need to impose or respond to discipline, enjoy each other's company and, if the grandparents have given up work, they can do so with that much less reservation, without jobs to preoccupy them.

The alternate generations can merge all the better when the older has left the ordinary occupational structure behind. Each generation, or set of generations, has its own demographic pattern. Our people belonged to one where marriage was early so that they also became grandparents early and some of them were already great-grandparents.

There was plenty of evidence of the warmth. Mr Stephens was exceptional, but not all that so, when he described what he did with his grandson. He was sixty-two years old, until two years ago a foreman at a boat builder's. He had a wife, and his daughter lived nearby. But they both worked full-time, leaving him, delightedly, to look after Peter, his grandson. On the day he described in his diary he fetched Peter from his daughter's before she left for her work, took him to playschool, took the dog for a walk, did some housework and started preparing the lunch, went to fetch Peter and played with him in the garden, finished the lunch in time for his wife when she came back home for it before returning to work, watched TV with Peter in the afternoon and played with him until his daughter came to fetch him on her way back from her work. His weekday life was a compound of his wife's but particularly his daughter's and his grandson's routines. If he was entrained by any one more than another it was by Peter. When he was asked whether he had got used to having free time and he replied, 'I haven't had much yet', there was no tinge of regret in his voice.

When she retired at sixty Mrs Trend did not find the same solace. She missed her work friends and did not have the company of her husband to make up for it because they were more or less the same age and he did not retire until he was sixty-five. In the interim she had been 'under the doctor' for depression. For the Trends there was some restabilisation when eventually he did give up. The routines of day and week for both of them were governed by their daughter's job and their consequent obligations as child-minders. On the diary day their daughter brought her children over to them at 8.15 so that Mr Trend could take them to school. They both picked up their grandchildren at 4 p.m., and then, while looking after the children, prepared the dinner for their daughter and her husband so that it was ready for them to eat as soon as they got home from work. The two grandparents stayed on to do the washing up before returning to their own beds in their own house. The next day Mr Trend gave each of his grandsons some books he had bought for them the previous day in the street market. They all had time to look through the books and talk about them before driving off to school. During the morning the two of them happily deputised for the parents by attending a concert at the school in honour of the retiring headmistress.

It was much the same with the Barleys. 'We do everything together.' With six sons and already eight grandchildren what need had they of friends? 'It's mostly family now', said Mr Barley 'It's enough.' One of his grandsons came to stay every Monday and, as that was the night when Mr Barley was interviewed, the boy listened in while idling contentedly on the sofa. The family may have stayed so close because Mr Barley – a retired postman – used to run two boys' football teams that his sons played for. Football had preserved the shape of his week. He went with some of his sons to watch Charlton Athletic whenever they were playing at home, followed by the traditional evening pints and, on the following day, the traditional Sunday roast. The pension from the Post Office, though low, was not so low that he could no longer afford a joint of beef.

Mrs Cream we have mentioned earlier in the chapter. We interviewed her for a second time a year later. Aided by her two motorbikes, she had persevered with her job as a coach-attendant and kept it despite a series of operations. But finally everything became too much for her and she suffered a nervous breakdown following the death of her mother. Her working life ended with eight weeks in hospital. Stopping work made her sad and guilty. 'I felt I was letting the kids down. Many of them have great writing difficulties and yet every one of the kids on the coach signed the card.' It took a lot of badgering by her husband, children and doctor to persuade her to retire; she felt she would rather crawl to work than give it up. Her family's concern was that she had worn herself out and needed rest. This was no doubt the case – but since stopping work her life had been much as before. A round of activities with the children and the many grandchildren (eleven so far) filled the days from 7 a.m. onwards – she didn't by any means always find time for the afternoon rest she was now supposed to take. As with many of the women in our sample (and the wives of the men interviewed), Mrs Cream's relatives quickly became accustomed to having her around and available. A typical day involved getting one grandson up at a quarter to seven, giving him breakfast and seeing him off to school before taking her husband his tea in bed. Babysitting for another grandson throughout a day punctuated by many phone calls from various offspring was followed by more visiting of family members right through to the evening, when it was back home to prepare her husband's dinner and spend the remainder of a full day with him.

Work ending for Mrs Cream had meant neither release into a life of relaxation nor a sentence of empty days and boredom. In her case the breakdown of her health meant that *something* had to go, and paid work was the only activity her family (if not Mrs Cream herself) could pinpoint as expendable. She was certainly in no danger of feeling useless. Mrs Cream herself was confident that the family could cope without her constant attention, and perhaps should; she had begun to decorate her house (despite her rheumatism, arthritis and angina) in accordance with her plan to sell up and move with her husband to a flat in Spain. She was typical of a number of women we interviewed who, though they preferred a paid job, had busy lives largely because they had other people, and particularly grandchildren, to look after.

Mrs Eames was one of these. She visited her daughter every day. On the first of the two diary days she arrived at 1.15, did some ironing for her, took her daughter's dog for a walk, tidied up her garden and was waiting for her when she came home herself at 5 p.m. with the grandson. On the second day she went with her daughter to take the grandson to an out-patient clinic at the hospital. She returned to the daughter's for lunch and the afternoon proceeded as it had the day before.

Mrs Andrews looked after her grandson every day. Her daughter went out to work. 'I'm now studying my grandson', she says. 'I had to push my own out at three months. The child is a real comfort and joy.' On her first diary day she made the breakfast at 7.45, ate it with the baby, watched TV with the baby, took the baby out for a bit of air, did some shopping. At 9.45 she put the baby to sleep, then did a crossword. At 11.45 she woke him up and gave him a drink and then again they watched TV together. At 12.15 they had lunch. After playing with him she put him down to sleep at 2.15. At 3.45 she changed and fed him. At 4.30 she began to prepare the evening meal so that it was all ready when her daughter got home. The second day was all the same except in the morning she took the baby to the doctor. She wrote: '5 p.m. – the evening starts when the mother takes the child from me. The baby has a time clock in him; he's my time piece now.'

But lest it be thought that all is always warmth and happiness, Mr and Mrs Duke showed how much it could be the opposite. They also looked after their grandson every day. The boy, aged three, was continually asking questions. But whenever he did so while the interviewer was there, the boy was slapped. He was obviously used to it because he showed no outward emotion whatsoever. Between 8 a.m. when his mother left him and 5.15 when she collected him again there was very little for him to do except put up with the slaps.

The Dukes were highly unusual amongst our sample. In general people's role as grandparents seemed to bring satisfaction, as much to the grandfathers as to the grandmothers; sometimes even more so if when their own children were young they had been so busy with their work that they had barely seen them grow up or had been held back from intimacy by the belief that looking after children was 'women's business'. After retirement they were having their first first-hand experience of rearing children. The second chance could be all the more precious if they had missed the first.

But they could miss out again if they did not have the money. Whether people could keep in touch with grandchildren and with other relatives depended on where they lived and, if more than walking distance away, on whether they had cars. Very few of the unemployed (being generally worse off than the retired) could afford them. Others had given them up and seen a good deal less of relatives as a result. Mr Pollitt used to see his older son and his children frequently; without a car it was down to twice a year.

Where our informants had held on to their cars they could

more readily hold on to their families. Mrs Cunliffe looked after her mother who was an invalid in Orpington. To do so Mr Cunliffe had to go there twice every day, to take his wife in the morning and pick her up again in the evening. In between he worked on his car! Mr and Mrs Bowles on one of the days recorded in their diary first shopped in Woolwich, then went to Blackheath to visit a son and then to Greenwich Hospital to see a sister.

Salience of the family

Such evidence as we have on the part played by grandfathers and grandmothers suggested that the family (for those that had one) bulked even larger in their lives than in the past. This is partly due to the same underlying convergence between the sexes. Where once men were almost strangers to their families, being in their homes no more than was necessary to eat and sleep, more and more men have been spending almost as much time there as their wives. Of our two metaphors the cable has therefore become less apt for men, and the cat's cradle, with its complexities, tensions and joys, more so. This has a direct bearing on our main theme. For it follows that whether or not people were active rather than passive third agers was bound to depend on their activities and the contrasts between them not only outside the family but also inside it, and between the outside and the inside. With the kind of data we had we could not show how many people who would otherwise have been in the passive category moved into the active one by virtue of their activity within the family and the outside activities to which their families introduced them. Most people's lives were too much all of a piece for that. But it was obvious from one account after another how much their families mattered to them. The family helped to make many people, who would anyway have been in our active category, even more so and helped to put many people into the active category who would otherwise not have been in it at all. It also protected the time-structure of some of the people who would otherwise have been passive. This last was particularly true of women. As we saw in the last chapter, none of them had time-structures which had collapsed.

If we cannot be precise about what the presence of a family meant for men, can we say anything firm about its absence? Not many were without a spouse or child or other close relative, and some of those who were and had been single for a long time, or even all their lives, seemed to manage perfectly well. They were used to living alone. Not so the people who had lived with a partner and lost them recently. Some of them could not get used to it at all. The Mr Groom of the last chapter – the man with the ageing dog – was one of these, Mr Hastings another. His experience showed that if you are to get divorced, do it earlier when there is a better chance of remarrying. Everything about the divorce in his early sixties had been painful: the parting; the divorce itself which was long-drawn-out, with almost no direct communication with his wife; the alienation from his son who sided with his mother and still came round regularly not out of kindness but to keep the quarrel going; and having to vacate his home for his wife and son. He had left behind a great deal of himself, including the telescope and other equipment with which he had cultivated his main hobby, astronomy. There was no room for it in the small bed-sit to which he had been reduced, in a house occupied by one other old man on his own. Losing his job not long after losing his wife was a further shock even though a lesser one. Mr Sawyer, divorced and alone, was a bit better off but only on the strength of the fairly elaborate survival tactics described before. There were others like him who found a double bereavement – in marriage and in work – particularly hard to bear.

*　　*　　*

We would like to end this chapter by stressing the difference that the new kind of family has made to men who have one. Not so long ago men – especially working-class men – kept themselves away from 'women's work' and therefore had only a meagre role in the family either before or after retirement. What could be thought an advantage for some of them while they were working was most definitely not when they stopped.

Their lot used to be miserable. Old men were treated almost as strangers within the home. Townsend said in 1957 of the old men he studied:

> Competent wives and competent daughters did not need them in the home. 'The wife always used to have the place on her own. They get grumpy if you get in their way. "I want to do this", she'll say. "What you doing here?" and you have to get out . . . You see some of the old 'uns. It's like penal servitude. They come out about nine in the morning and don't go home till five in the afternoon' . . . This was why so many men talked of retirement as a tragedy. They were forced to recognise that it was not their working life which was over, it was their life. 'In the sweat of thy face shalt thou eat bread till thou return unto the ground.'*

That has changed, and not only in Greenwich. Insofar as feminism has been the dynamic behind the growth of the symmetrical family, the greatest beneficiaries of feminism have not been women of any age but old men. This great change has not had to wait until the young bearing the new ideas have become old but has moved ahead of them, as a bow-wave moves ahead of a ship. The young women who have made the wave roll have been the benefactors of the old men. The greater solidarity of the family at later ages is an advantage to men who, dying younger than their wives, have someone to look after them. In approaching death they are not so alone. But for many women in their seventies and eighties the family has become completely asymmetrical. Such women represent the triumph of the new demography; but they are often as alone as older men once were in the asymmetrical families of the past. It is as though older men have been decimated in a war, leaving their widows behind them, and no one yet knows how the slaughter of the men can be prevented.

Men are more engaged in the family than they were just as women are more engaged in paid work. The changes presented

* P. Townsend, *The Family Life of Old People – An Inquiry in East London,* p.147.

in this chapter – the older women in the labour market, older men being pushed down into the bottom jobs where women used to be exploited on their own, the sharing in the home, the re-uniting of husbands and wives after they both retire, the respect given in the home to older men who had very little of it in the past – these have all contributed to the making of a new kind of family which, despite the continuing industrial revolution, still survives strongly. The family stands apart from, and contrasts with, the economy in dozens of different ways, and not least in the kind of time it keeps.

Family time is not the same as industrial time. The clock and the calendar of industry and the State are almost as meticulously imposed on it as on every other institution in a high-technology society. But the family slips away a little; it still belongs more to nature – to the biological rhythms of sleep and hunger and sex and the slow maturing of children and the slow decline of age – than to the new metronomic society in which everything else is measured out with so much brisk pride. There is no cut-off point in family time just because people give up their ordinary jobs outside it. People do not give up each other in the family because they have given up their friends from work. The pre-industrial family has, as we pointed out before, lost some of its main functions to the State, the ordinary workplace and the school. But it can come into its own when paid work is over for the day and when it is over for the life. When people leave the other institutions behind, the family is there to fall back on. It is the opposite of the limited liability company; it can be the unlimited liability company.

SIX

No *Hardening* of the Categories

'I wish to be somebody, not nobody; a
doer – deciding, not being decided for.'
Isaiah Berlin, Oxford

It is hard to believe that any 149 people, even though chosen at random, could be so different. The joyous and the depressed, the intensely active and those with time hanging on their hands; some busily engaged with the great society well beyond Greenwich and others barely creeping from a house in one street to a house in another and back again; the straight-backed and the arthritic; those whose chief delight is playing with two-year-olds and others who dread seeing a child again; those who have never been on a holiday and those who drive to their caravan at Clacton almost every weekend; those whose only routine is watching cricket in the summer and football in the winter and others who tend their chrysanthemums every day; those who look forward to Lammas-tide and others who have not been in a church since they were married – they are all here. It is cramping to pack them between two covers, let alone into any Age.

But they all belong to a society which has enjoyed a demographic revolution, even if it has not yet enjoyed it as much as the society could. Had the expectation of life been declining, this book would not have been written. The number of people over retirement age would have been falling away, any third age on the way to extinction. As it is, with the expectation of life increasing as a result of higher standards of living bringing better nutrition, better public health measures and better medical practice, the third age is expanding rather than contracting.

Our main enquiry, since all our third agers have the negative freedom of no paid work, has been into how many of them enjoy the positive freedom of making something of it. So far as we know, no numbers have been given before. The precise figures we arrived at – roughly two to one in favour of the negative third agers as against the positive – are not so significant in themselves. They would become more so if a like attempt at a classification were made in other enquiries, in different places and at different times.* Had our sample been of older people than those we had, we would expect more of them to show up as negative. But if the proportions in any fresh enquiries were anywhere near ours it would show how little cause for satisfaction there is and how far we still have to go before we can say that older people are getting what they could of a positive nature from a stage of life that may well last a quarter of a century or more.

As well as asking about the sheer numbers we have set out some of the characteristics of the people on each side of the line. The most striking fact was that the positive people were engaged in activities which, in a way, resembled what they had done before. Many of them were engaged in 'work', although not paid work. A few had only one unpaid occupation, although they could be quite as absorbed in it as in any paid one, as Mr Penny was by his horses, Mr Sutcliffe by his church or Mr Howard by his genealogy. But most had several part-time unpaid jobs, and the variety was, as we have said, something that specially distinguished these people. Professor Handy (whom we have already quoted) suggested, when giving evidence to the same House of Commons Committee,** that the older people get, the more variety they need, and that having several jobs – what he called a 'portfolio' of different bits of work – was for many the most satisfactory arrangement. If unpaid jobs are counted our informants bear this out. Some of their portfolios included personal hobbies as well as a voluntary job in a church or some other organisation.*** This variety may itself go a long way to

---

* For another approach, based principally on research into French *préretraites*, see Xavier Gaullier, *La Deuxième Carrière: âges, emplois, retraites*.

** House of Commons Employment Committee, *The Employment Pattern of the Over 50s*, Vol. 1, p.126.

*** In the EC '40 million people claimed to be not merely members but to be actively working for a range of voluntary organisations'. Michael Fogarty, *Meeting the Needs of the Elderly*, p.80.

explain why many of them found the unpaid more satisfying than the single paid job they had had before. Perhaps it would have been better still if they had had a paid part-time job as well. But even as it was, they had moved from a singular into a plural society of their own making, a plural society to which some of the women picked out in Chapter 5 have belonged for a long time.

Their time-structures were more flexible than when they had been in ordinary jobs. But the structure was still made up of routines and contrasts, even if the patterns were more complex than they had been. The juxtaposition of recurrences and discontinuities, the same and the different, constituted the order which people needed. This was shown both by those who had the structure, and, even more strikingly, by those who did not. In Chapter 4 we picked out, amongst the general body of the negative third agers, those whose time-structure had collapsed. For them the new freedom really was a tragic gift, a burden to be borne with some stoicism perhaps, but a burden all the same, not an opportunity to be seized and enjoyed. Making yourself wait patiently for 11.30 to treat yourself to a treacle sandwich is not how anyone would imagine the new Jerusalem. Yet we do not expect the Sawyers to point the way to the future so much as the Prendergasts.

Will the future be so different from the present pattern if all that happens is that unpaid work replaces paid work? In Chapter 4 we argued that it would not be so very different, not only because paid work is bound to cast its shadow forward but, more significantly, because paid and unpaid work, and any other kind of existence, have to satisfy the fundamental human need to deal with the passage of time by blending habit with the contrast which makes room for the unexpected. It is only contrast and the surprise of the unexpected which can keep at bay the boredom which is modern society's greatest bane. If ordinary work becomes less dominant in the next century, as we expect it will, new kinds of people may emerge in large numbers who are less ready to put up with repetition in their lives than has been customary so far. The boundaries of positive liberty may be pushed brilliantly outwards without producing widespread psychological destabilisation. But even without that happening, without the limits set by the habit-contrast duo being substantially relaxed, there is still room for a good deal more variation, and if that occurs amongst older people more and more of them will qualify for a positive third age. This is crucial to our general argument. Older people who have given up work constitute an age-class and a growing one. But that age-class could be socially inert unless it embodies enough of a distinctive way of life to mark it off from people of conventional working age. We think it is clear that some older people are already playing that distinctive role, and if still more of them do, and if many of them are less specialists than generalists (as we also expect them to be), the major trend towards ever greater specialisation and fragmentation that has been driven so hard since the industrial revolution could come to a stop.

The State and the Third Age

The outcome will also depend upon State policy, and the first issue is the one raised in Chapter 3 about early retirement. It matters so much because the pensionable ages settled by the State have become generalised in the private occupational schemes which the State has encouraged by tax benefits. The State's ages were laid down at a time when to a large extent they controlled the exit from the labour force, through the State's direct power and its indirect influence. There was a match between policy and practice. But as we have seen, the matching has become less exact. Increasing numbers of people, men in particular, are leaving in their fifties before they get to the government's departure gate and without the support they would get if they stayed. People in their fifties could not be blamed for complaining, like Mr Gladstone, 'People of my age are in a backwater. They're spending millions on youth training but they don't take into account people of my generation. All of a sudden, crash-bang, you're on the scrapheap.'

The falling off in employment for men is not due to individual failings. They have been in the grip of a general shift which has had three principal manifestations.

1 The first of these is the social class polarisation which we have mentioned before. This arises partly out of the general improvement in health which, paradoxically, has kept alive many people who would not in the past have survived as far as their fifties, but in a poor state of health, and on that score alone not all that employable.

2 Conventional prejudice has also told against the old. Employers have been disinclined to change their recruiting practices not 'because older people have higher wage expectations, are less mobile or have a poorer health record, but that they are too set in their ways, hard to train and "do not fit in"; this despite evidence that, at least in office work, older people are more reliable and have less absenteeism'.* So employers have been inclined to sack older people rather than younger, making them less employable still, as teachers do with the same knock-on effect when they treat some children as failures. People who fail in competition with others become more and more likely to fail again. Nothing fails like failure. Any setback, any piece of bad luck, can set off a downward spiral wherever competitive pressures are strong enough. People can become conditioned to fail by the hostility of their social environment or, to be plainer about it, by the callousness of other people.

3 The labour market has reflected the change in industrial structure. The 'older' manufacturing industries have declined relative to the 'younger' service-based industries, and older people were employed disproportionately in the former. Employment in the metals and minerals sector dropped by nearly one third between 1981 and 1987.** In that sector three in ten of the workforce were over fifty, compared with one in four of those employed in all industries. In such industries not only have there been fewer jobs overall but, as the rate of industrial change has speeded up, older workers have as always had to bear the brunt of it. In so

* House of Commons Employment Committee, *The Employment Patterns of the Over 50s*, Vol.1, p.xi.
** R.M. Lindley and R.A. Wilson (eds), *Review of the Economy and Employment 1988–89 – Vol.1; Occupational Assessment*, p.11.

far as they are specialised, they date back to the structure of industry as it was when they entered it and as that has changed, their skills have become partially or wholly obsolete. More older workers would be employed if all-purpose skills were cultivated amongst people of all ages; and, indeed, more are being employed in the early 1990s because there is a shortage of the school-leavers on whom employers used to rely.* But with training, inadequate as it is, as much concentrated on the young as education, older workers are still liable to be caught in a time-warp which, for industry, mirrors what has happened to older people more generally in society.

The traditional view of what is 'old' has been quite irrelevant in this new situation and so far no British government has done more than fiddle with the problem. The result is that very large numbers of people have been caught in what we called the Age Trap. Everywhere people are at the same time being condemned by employers as too old to work and by the State as too young not to work. While some people get more affluent as they get older, others do the opposite. The Matthew effect – to them that hath – tells against older people even more sharply than it does against younger. The ever-present and growing danger is of an increasing polarisation between those already better-off, with fine pensions, choice about when to retire, a range of opportunities for paid and unpaid work and an easy acceptance of their past and present status in a solidly male gerontocracy on the one hand, and on the other the marginalised people who are impoverished and insecure, without access to paid work, striving if they can to earn a few pounds in the black economy.

* The views of employers and the government about the merits of older people have been liable to cyclical swings in the past, with the merits being played up in booms when labour is short and played down in recessions when labour is more plentiful. In 1950, when labour was in particularly short supply, the Parliamentary Secretary to the Minister of Labour said 'I have no doubt that many people would have a happier and healthier old age if they continue in their work a little longer rather than give up their routine and sink into a premature old age'. Quoted in C. Phillipson, *Capitalism and the Construction of Old Age*, p.88.

This situation is manifestly unjust, especially when it is so chancy whether a person is unemployed, an invalid or early retired. The way out is to extend State financial support for earlier retirement and at the same time to encourage more employment (especially part-time) for older people. Such proposals are not in the least incompatible with our advocacy of the third age. On the contrary, if earlier retirement were encouraged, and supported, that should increase the numbers in the third age. Fewer people like those in Chapter 3 would be compelled to consider themselves as in the labour force when there was in effect no place for them within it.

The most sweeping change with this end in view would be to bring the pensionable age right down to, say, fifty for both men and women, not as the age when anyone had to retire but as the age when they could retire if they wished. It may come to that eventually. But for the moment the cost would be prohibitive, placing too great a burden on younger employed people, and so in the short term we need to settle for something less costly. Raising the disability benefits and invalidity allowances would help those whose health was too poor to enable them to continue actively in full-time employment. But that would not benefit the rest, nor change the present fact that once older people become unemployed they remain in that state so much longer than others.

The present practice is that unemployed men over sixty can receive a Pension Premium in addition to their basic Income Support. Their National Insurance contributions are also credited to them so that they do not lose out in any way on their eventual entitlement to an ordinary pension. The practice should be extended downwards in age so that the Pension Premium would be made available to men and women over fifty who have been unemployed continuously for more than, say, six months. They should also get the travel, health service and other concessions for which only ordinary pensioners are eligible at the moment. To achieve its effect on well-being the benefit would need a name which dissociated it both from unemployment and from Income Support which has a pejorative tone to it; it could well be called (following the practice in the Ford factory and elsewhere) an Early Retirement Pension. The ordinary pension would replace the Early Retirement Pension once people had reached ordinary pensionable age.*

Age-discrimination

Whatever else is done, part-time and full-time employment for older people should be encouraged and this could be done by legislation against the age discrimination which is at present so rife. A change of attitude is badly needed, and it would be stimulated, as the House of Commons Committee said, 'if those who have the power to determine employment policies in the private and public sectors bothered to look in the mirror. If they are not too old at 50 neither are others'.** But if it was going to happen through mirror-watching it would have happened already. A push from outside is needed.

The experience of the United States is to the point. There the campaign against age-discrimination, or ageism as it is more often called, originated in the civil rights movement of the 1960s. The Civil Rights Act of 1964 prohibited employment discrimination based on race, sex, religion or national origin. Should it also be banned on grounds of age? The Secretary of Labor was asked to investigate and report to Congress, which he did a year later. He found age discrimination widespread. Almost half the

* Sweden has an early pension which encourages part-time employment, although not at as early an age as we are proposing for the Early Retirement Pension. 'The success of such schemes relies on an adequate supply of part-time employment for older people and Swedish experience shows that this goal can be achieved. It is also important, if the scheme is to be attractive to older people, for partial pensions to be counted as pensionable income. The part-time/partial pension scheme covers the age range 60–65; in order to qualify an individual must work at least 5 hours less than the normal full-time working week, but at least 17 hours per week . . . Research in Sweden shows substantial benefits from the partial retirement scheme: increase in ability amongst mature workers to retain employment, an improvement in their health and a decline in absenteeism. At the same time employers report that partial pensioners are more productive than full-time employees. They are also less likely than full-time workers of the same age to become disabled or unemployed.' T. Schuller and A. Walker, *The Time of Our Life: Education, Employment and Retirement in the Third Age*, pp.16–17.
** House of Commons Employment Committee, *The Employment Pattern of the Over 50s*, Vol.1. p.x.

vacancies in the private sector were reserved for those under fifty-five. New legislation was recommended and the Age Discrimination in Employment Act was passed in 1967. In its approach it followed some of the more successful State laws which relied on persuasion more than legal sanctions, although as an ultimate recourse they were provided for. The purpose of the Act was:

> to promote employment of older workers based on their ability rather than age; to prohibit age discrimination in employment; to help employers and workers find ways of meeting problems arising from the impact of age on employment.

Its coverage extended from the age of forty up to sixty-five, despite the fact that stating any age was itself discriminatory. Unions were within its scope as well as employers, so that it would, for example, be illegal for them to enter into any agreement for early retirement or redundancy where age was the criterion for selection.

The Act had and has shortcomings. Age discrimination is still prevalent in the American work-place. Even today few people in the USA are even aware that the statute exists.* But such legislation has been of some value and, if followed up with a vigorous campaign, could make the sort of age-discrimination reported in this book less common. It would be as illegal to rule out people from a job, dismiss them or fail to promote them on account of age alone as it is already to do so on grounds of gender or ethnic origin.**

---

* See F. Laczko and C. Phillipson, 'Age Discrimination in Employment'.
** It should certainly apply well beyond ordinary employment. Eric Midwinter has pointed out that the Citizens' Advice Bureaux have not taken on any volunteers over sixty-five and retirement at seventy has been obligatory; St John's Ambulance Brigade has not accepted volunteers of over sixty-five; county and local WRVS have ruled out people over sixty-five for positions of responsibility; guides and scouts in uniform have not wanted people over sixty-five; and so it goes on. E. Midwinter, 'Your Country Doesn't Need You!'

Sex discrimination – against men

Another change is also needed which would end a form of discrimination against men which dates back to the Hitler war. In retrospect it seems a kind of mistake, or aberration, in social policy to have done what the government did in 1940 when it departed from equality and reduced the State pension age for women from sixty-five (which it had been since 1925 when it was reduced from seventy) to sixty. The main prompt was the goodwill created by the contribution of women to the war effort and the wish to show them appreciation, although of a kind that was to be paid for by posterity rather than during the war itself. The measure was a kind of post-war credit for women. A further argument was that men usually married women younger than themselves – itself a practice deriving from a period of unchallenged male ascendancy – and so couples would more often be able to retire together, or nearly together, if there was an age stagger for retirement.

It never did make much sense. It has made even less as older women have increased their presence in the labour force, as men have reduced theirs so that more men have been without either job or pension, and as women have continued to outlive men by a growing margin. 'The Third Age is to a considerable extent a feminine affair everywhere, and becomes more so as years of later life slip by.'* But the disparity is more and more called in question by the shift towards symmetry described in the previous chapter and the ideology which is both cause and consequence of the shift. The most telling impetus towards greater equality has come from the Common Market. After the European Court ruled against different compulsory retirement ages for men and women, the UK Sex Discrimination Act was passed and came into force in 1987. It made it unlawful to dismiss a woman on grounds of age where a man would not have been. The effect of it has been felt first by private occupational pension schemes which are moving over to common retirement ages. 'A recent CBI survey, covering 260 schemes, showed that 57 per cent of firms are now operating common retirement ages, with two-

* P. Laslett, *A Fresh Map of Life*, p.39.

thirds of these having newly introduced them as a result of the Act.'* The practice has been for women's ages to be raised to sixty-five.

With the change gathering momentum, and more pressure coming from the European Court, the government cannot hold back for much longer from removing the discrimination against men. It should not be done by lowering the pension age of men to sixty. That would not only be very costly indeed, especially now that the earnings rule has been abolished so that people can draw their pension *and* have a job and incidentally contribute more to tax revenues. It would also be to flout all that we have been saying throughout the book about the rising expectation of life. As the span of active life increases it would make no sense at all to encourage people to leave work earlier than they have been doing by reducing the age for a full ordinary pension for men. On the contrary, we hope that more people will be willing to do paid work, particularly in part-time jobs, until later than has been customary – this even though we know that for most people paid work will not have the primacy it has had in the past. So we are left with only one way of achieving equality, that is by raising the pension age for women to sixty-five. The shift upwards would have to be very gradual. Women who in their later years are looking forward to drawing their pensions at sixty cannot suddenly have their legitimate expectations frustrated. But even though the levelling-up process is eased in over a transitional period it will represent a further move towards the convergence between the sexes which was the subject of Chapter 5. When a single age comes into force,** the symmetry between the sexes will in this respect at least be complete. There will also be more symmetry in the composition of the third age.

* Confederation of British Industry, 'Flexible Retirement Policies and Equality in Pension Provision: a CBI Strategy'. House of Commons Employment Committee, *The Employment Patterns of the Over 50s*, Vol. II, p.73. P. Carroll also confirms that occupational pension schemes have been moving quickly towards equalisation at the age of sixty-five. *Pension Age in a Changing Society*, p.22.
** The issue was well discussed by P. Tompkins in *Flexibility and Fairness – a study in equalisation of pension ages and benefits*. Tompkins came to a different conclusion not about the principle but about the way to honour it.

Second education system needed

The reduction in the pension age for men and financial support for the early retirement of more people in their fifties, both of which we have been advocating, would between them add still further to the numbers of people in the third age but would not necessarily do anything for their quality of life. The ratio between the active and the passive could stay obstinately the same. Whether it does so, or improves, will depend, amongst other things, on the effort put into education and training. Training is relevant because it could help more older people stay in work – highly desirable if that is what they want – but also help them in their new third-age careers.

Government policy on training has concentrated – almost exclusively – on the young, on the grounds that the money spent on older people is liable to be wasted because they will so soon be leaving the labour force. This is for once much too long-sighted; the pace of change in the work-place is so fast that any training becomes fairly quickly obsolete. Laslett has suggested that the longest an updated training can last is ten years.* If so, it follows that a worker who was trained or re-trained at the age of fifty-five could have the same ten years to go (in their case before retiring) as anyone else. But if retirement from ordinary full-time work were regarded as no more than an artificial cut-off point, or as no more than the point in life when the balance between paid and unpaid work was going to change, any training at almost any time in later life could turn out to be useful. The training needs to be as much for the 'voluntariat'** as for people in ordinary paid jobs.

But the expansion needed in training opportunities for older people is of small moment compared to the expansion needed in education which is not tied in any way to a particular job, paid or unpaid. As things are at present, older people are hardly touched. One estimate found only two per cent of those over sixty involved in any form of education*** and amongst those

* P. Laslett, *A Fresh Map of Life*, p.187.
** The term is used by Michael Fogarty in *Meeting the Needs of the Elderly*, p.92.
*** See E. Midwinter, *Age is Opportunity*.

(it is worth noting) women predominate. There have been some bright spots. The University of the Third Age was mentioned at the beginning of the book. As an institution in which all those who receive education are in principle also educators, it is expanding steadily. The Open University has also set itself out to attract older people, with more than three thousand students over the age of sixty in 1985.* The Open College of the Arts, as a little sister of the Open University, has also tried to recruit older people for the study of the arts and crafts, including photography, garden design and writing. Of the first seven thousand students of OCA some third were over fifty-five. Many local education authorities have within their limited resources also done a good deal for older people.

But without some specific support from the government little headway is going to be made to prepare older people for all they could do for themselves and others. The same Report of the House of Commons Committee that we have already cited was attracted to Professor Handy's proposal that anyone over fifty should have the right to educational credits which would entitle them to one year's training or education at any institution which they could persuade to take them. The Committee recommended a much modified and cheaper version of this proposal. One of the authors of this book has suggested something very similar – an entitlement of up to one year full-time (or equivalent part-time) in higher or further education to all those over fifty who have not yet had it and whose income and assets are below a certain level.** Such a scheme would therefore be tilted in favour of the less well-off with the advantage of offering special help to the kind of people we have put in the negative category.

We would like to point out a possible link between such educational vouchers – for that is the term we prefer – to one of the findings we noted in Chapter 4, about the importance attached to leaving ceremonies. Some substitute is clearly needed for the employers who accepted this responsibility in the past. Such ceremonies belonged to a more stable economy in which people stayed in one job, with one employer, for long periods.

* Quoted in T. Schuller, *Education and the Third Age*, p.11.
** T. Schuller, *Education and the Third Age*, p.14.

The employer could then look after both the employee's interests and his own – reassuring others who had not yet reached retirement age that they would be properly treated when their turn came – and also the interests of society. The employer organised the ritual occasion which could ease the transition between two stages of life. But as labour mobility has increased, with many people only staying with their last employer for a few months, or a year or so, it would be unreasonable to expect the employer to make much, if any, fuss over the departure of the newcomers. The responsibility needs to be rearranged and it would be particularly fitting if a ceremony when a person starts drawing a pension were used for the presentation of education vouchers by the granting body. Such a ceremony would then face towards the future rather than only commemorating the past. As well as a leaving ceremony it would also be a starting ceremony. It could be as much of a party as the retiring person wanted it to be, with as many relatives, friends and former workmates as he or she wanted to invite.

A second educational system for the third age will be required, with different characteristics from the first school-age system. Its ethos will be different, not designed to sharpen young people for the competitive world they are going to be thrown into but to prepare older people for a rather different style of life, with the emphasis on co-operation and self-development. It will need its own 'schools', not so much institutions as stimulating resource centres and mutual-aid learning circles. The vouchers would also entitle older people to join in any of the classes of what have up till now been the orthodox schools, colleges and universities of the country – this as a step towards detaching educational institutions from serving the interests of one age-group alone. A third-age careers advisory service will also be needed to act as a clearing-house for information on paid and unpaid jobs for older workers, as a counselling service, a promoter of part-time work, a guide on training and, generally, an ally of this new parallel education system.

It would, of course, be costly, but for those who would demur on these grounds we present three arguments. First, there is the case for intergenerational justice. The vast majority of our sample left school at fifteen or earlier and never benefited from the huge post-war expansion of education. Three out of four of our Greenwich sample had left school at fourteen or under, a further one in ten before fifteen. Whatever disappointment there has been about the impact of that expansion on social equality or educational achievement, they never had the chance even to try themselves out. Secondly, there is the prevention of greater costs. 'Use it or lose it' is the motto of pre-retirement education, referring to physical and mental ability. The cost of *not* providing opportunity is not easy to quantify with any degree of precision but it will certainly be huge as the population ages, with more people falling into our third age. Thirdly, there is the loss of economic output from a more highly experienced labour force. Society loses by failing to allow older people to work if they want to, unpaid or paid. The loss is compounded by failing to provide these older workers with more advanced skills. A skilled voluntariat could be almost as cost-beneficial to the country as a whole as a skilled workforce of the ordinary sort.

The more fundamental reform

Up to this point in the chapter we have not been questioning in any radical way the age-stratification to which we drew attention in Chapter 1. But, third age or no third age, the division into age-classes cannot be regarded as an ordinance that has to be observed for all time. It is a fact of nature that people age: for insurance purposes no better statistic has been found for determining the probability of death than a person's age. But it is not a fact of nature that there is only one way of ageing or one pace of ageing, or that human beings have to be organised around the age imputed to them. Age-stratification is a device invented by society, not by nature. Society was not like this before the industrial revolution and it is not like that in parts of the world not fully in the grip of industrialisation.

So the question is, does industrialisation, if not human nature, make it inevitable that social organisation should pivot so much on age as it does? We do not deny that what has been done has become entrenched, even though the ballooning out of the first age and the third age is already undermining the age-based society and will (we think) undermine it completely before long. The age-principle has helped to keep people head down in their stations in life. A vast array of institutional expectations of how people should behave at different ages has been created. On the whole people have conformed to them, obediently filling out the role of a 3-year-old, a 23-year-old, a 43-year-old or a 73-year-old and always in competition, as well as companionship, with people of more or less their own age. Before the arrival of industry, the presence and the threat of hunger were almost enough to discipline people when allied to the authority embodied in the ordinary class system. The relaxing of hunger as a sanction made it necessary to find other devices for keeping people in order and, for this purpose, the age-principle has been a vital reinforcement for acquisitiveness. The principle has been all the more credible because it appears to come straight from nature. We all get older and if the fact cannot be denied it has not been all that convincing to reject the social organisation which derives from it. Unless another like fact of nature – the differences between the sexes – had been challenged in the way it applied to social behaviour, age-stratification would not in its turn have become so open to challenge.

We have in the course of this study become more and more aware of the artificiality of this kind of age-stratification. It has seemed more and more paradoxical – a central paradox of modern society – that so much has been done, so effectively, to reduce the injury done to people by biological ageing and so little the injury done by social ageing. In the next century most people in the richer countries of the world could live till they die without too much pain, too much suffering and too much impairment of their faculties. But the damage done to people by social ageing has not been reduced; it has been increased and could continue to increase.

It has not happened as part of any grand design, consciously thought out. The column has been marching briskly ahead, flags flying, drumsticks rattatting, bugles blowing, but composed of the blind. If there has been any plan to the march it has come from the dark depths of sociology where there are no intentions, only consequences. But the State *has* been the indispensable instrument without which the entry-ports and the exit-ports to the parade ground would not have been guarded by such meticulous arithmeticians with such majesty of law to back them up. Every blind girl and blind old man has had to pin their age to a placard on their backs so that the keepers with their telescopic arms, as blind except to numbers as any computer, can bar one from entry and the other from re-entry.

And how wretched some of the consequences can be! The people we described in Chapter 3 were discriminated against by employers and prevented by the State from drawing any proper support until they had reached a quite arbitrary age selected by a State determined to confine everyone to the same straitjacket. So it is with many others. People are publicly and privately humiliated on a millionfold scale by reason of their age, not just deprived of work and money because they are of the wrong age but shamed by being regarded by others as slow, rigid, unenterprising, incapable of innovation, intellectually decayed by reason of their age alone. Almost the worst of it is that the cruelty of others is internalised by those it is vented upon, so that they feel old and unworthy when they do not need to. Much of the suffering of the old is unnecessary, representing the psychological damage created by a social artefact which could in time be taken apart just as it was put together, piece by piece. The ageless society is just as noble a cause as the classless society; even if neither will ever be fully attainable that does not make them less worthwhile as objectives. The third age is itself an attempt to slacken the grip of society by improving the social image and hence the self-image of 'the old', and to make the question of how old anyone is more and more irrelevant to how they actually behave and are treated. It is worthwhile for that alone. The cause is worthwhile too because the suffering and embarrassment are not reserved for the old alone, even if they are the worst victims. It can strike at forty-year-olds, thirty-year-olds, even ten-year-olds.

A *radical new approach*

The particular reforms we discussed earlier in this chapter are (we consider) justifiable on their own merits and urgently needed. But we do not believe that in the longer run the unnecessary injury can be reduced in a decisive manner except by a radically new approach: regarding the ages of adults as something very personal to them, their private property, which they are entitled to privacy about, a private matter to be taken out of the public and placed in the private domain. This will require bringing age within the scope of an extended Data Protection Act which goes well beyond what is stored in computers: their age would become information which people would not be required to give to the State or anyone else nor others allowed to pass on without permission, except for census purposes where individuals would not be identified.

Big Brother will always be tempted to act Big Brother if he has the data necessary for controlling us. But everything could begin to change as soon as the rendering of ages unto Caesar is no longer regarded as part of the social contract between the individual citizen and the State. The opposition to such a reform will say that all we are proposing is an atavistic return to the situation that obtained in the past, or still does in simple societies, where not only is there no State to record people's ages but they do not even know their own ages, or care. That is true: we are. But just because a practice (or lack of practice) was followed in the past does not necessarily mean that it is faulty now.

The placing of the age of adults in the private domain would have several significant consequences. It is only for that reason it is proposed at all. First, for the pension system. State and occupational pensions start at particular ages, and it is unthinkable that it could be otherwise in any system which derives from the insurance principle. People pay contributions for so many years and (whether on a strict actuarial basis or not) they then draw benefits from a certain age. But the whole system has been breaking down, as our survey (and common knowledge) makes clear. Many people are leaving work of their own accord or at someone else's behest well before pensionable age is reached. In due course something radical will have to be done anyway.

Our solution is far-reaching, and surely no worse on that account. For pensions would have to be abandoned along with age-enumeration, at any rate collectively organised pensions tied to ages of eligibility. What would have to be done instead? Older people would still require support, but if age was no longer a precondition of entitlement the support could no longer be in the form of a pension. It would have to be on the basis of need. Older people would be entitled to decent benefits whenever they needed it, like people of any age whatsoever.

The objection to this is that, if no more were done, people would have to show they were in need before they could receive support. Everyone would in that case be subject to a means test and so older people would no longer be entitled to an income from the State as of right. But there is in principle a straight-forward way of meeting and (we think) overcoming the objection – that is, by introducing a Social Wage or National Dividend, to use two of the terms that have sometimes been used.

A Social Wage has not, as far as we know, been advocated before in order to eliminate both age discrimination and age privilege. It has more often been proposed as a means of simplifying the whole tax and benefit system. As things are at present in Britain and every other industrial country, a vast bureaucracy is maintained in order to take money away from people in taxes according to rules of the utmost complexity that only a qualified accountant can fully understand; and in order to make over to people a series of payments in support of their incomes according to rules of such complexity that many of the beneficiaries do not understand, and therefore do not receive, the amounts to which they are entitled. Any alternative system of support could not be introduced at a stroke. It would be constructed detail by detail. But in principle a Social Wage would go a long way to ending that extraordinary multiplicity of payments from and to citizens. The Wage would be enough to live on, even if at a modest level. Whatever the level decided upon, it would be paid to each individual adult whether it was needed or not, just as pensions are now paid to both rich and poor. But it would be taxable as part of a person's income so that wealthier people would in effect return the Wage to the Exchequer in the form of taxes. There would still be a payment out and a payment in, but as part of a much simpler transaction than there is now, and there would be no means test for old people or anyone else except that which belongs by its very nature to income tax.

The proposal is put forward in the interests primarily of older people. But since at various points in this book we have coupled the old with the young – both subject to the same overarching bureaucracy of age – we should make it clear that we are not speaking just of the old. The young have to be involved too, if only because if any serious attempt is to be made to tackle ageism it cannot leave out the schools where people are indoctrinated in the values of the whole ageist society. The obedience by ordinary people to age starts in the school and is carried over even into old age. Attitudes will not change unless schools do.

The difference between the old and the young is that young children with their short experience of life cannot be expected to know what is best for them and so decide on their own whether to go to school or not. Nor do we see why the parents should be able to decide that their children should have no education and go to work instead, maybe to work *for* the parents. So the sole remaining ageist compulsion would be that children would have to start school at five or before. It would hardly seem a compulsion to the great majority of children since they are generally partial to primary schools, which teach so many things like numeracy and literacy which seem relevant to them. The troubles start in secondary schools with their specialisation which so often forfeits the interest of children.

So we see no good reason to compel pupils to remain in secondary school until they are sixteen. If as teenagers they have no wish to stay on and only do so because they are forced to, they are not likely to get anything much of value out of it themselves and they may by their very presence make it a good deal more difficult for other children and for teachers. The stock image is of a six-foot boy – almost a man in appearance – crammed into a school-desk and looking up with complete blankness, or even hostility, at a young woman teacher who is struggling to hold his interest and that of other more amenable pupils, and generally keep order. She can be faced with an almost impossible task. It surely makes more sense to give the option to young people to leave school if they wish to do so, and to settle on the age of thirteen, which has the justification that this is now around about the general age of puberty, as we pointed out in Chapter 1. From that time on, all information about their ages would be out of government records at Somerset House and elsewhere* and from that age they could enter upon the sort of training which Britain needs to provide so much more abundantly, or get a full-time job, or a part-time one coupled with part-time school, or a job doing public service for which they would receive payment. Clearly the young people could not be just thrown on their own resources. They will need the best regular advice and counselling they can get from a new careers and training service but always with the difference from their previous situation, that they would not be subject to the compulsion of the law.

The pressure would be on secondary schools to make themselves as stimulating and congenial as they could in order to persuade children to stay on voluntarily. So as to make it quite clear that anyone leaving school at thirteen would not forfeit their chances to a later education, all who left, and indeed also all who stayed on at school beyond thirteen, would be given vouchers entitling them to eight further years of education at whatever age they wanted it, from fourteen onwards. This scheme would eventually, after fifty years or so, replace the short-term education vouchers which we have suggested should be given to people when they start drawing a pension. Spending on education altogether would have to rise but the prize would

---

* When compulsory registration of births was first introduced in 1836 by Lord John Russell it all seemed very obvious. Speaking in the House of Commons he said, 'There might be some difficulties in the way of carrying out, to its full extent, a Bill of this nature at first. It might be the case with some persons that they would refuse to give the registrar the particulars he might require; but he (Lord J. Russell) was quite sure that where the plan was established, the advantages attending it would be so obvious, and would be so soon felt by all classes of persons, they would so soon perceive the benefit of having their children's names inserted in the general register, that it would not be very long before every one would be willing to concur in carrying out the plan.' Hansard, Vol.31, p.371, 12 February 1836. We are in favour of compulsory registration of births in order to ensure education up to the age of thirteen, but it is far from obvious why the State should hold on to the records for people of any age.

be very great: life-long education could at last become a fact instead of a dream.

The old and the young are under the sway of the State calculators in a way which people in between are not. But the same cramping and cribbing approach is adopted by many employers. People are continuously assessed by their age, being counted too young or too old for some post of responsibility or skill, and considered ripe for promotion or demotion according to the age they have reached rather than just by their competence. Large employers with sophisticated personnel departments carry age-ranking to ridiculous lengths and can (as we said in Chapter 1) settle the lifetime rank of an employee when the ceiling of what he or she can reach is lowered at the age of thirty, or twenty-one, or eighteen. The reform we are arguing for would make all that more or less impossible. Not that employers have to wait upon the State. They could alter their practice and move in the new direction without any change in the law, and so of course could individuals of any age who object to being age-tagged.

We have been dealing with the outward and visible manifestations of an attitude, and yet it is the attitude that must be our major concern. Our premise is that age has become one of the organising principles of modern society and as such has been carried so far as to inflict serious psychological injury on millions of people. Their age is used far more against people than it is for them: when it is brought up it is more often to blame than to praise. It is a common focus of criticism – that you are not performing well considering your age or that you should *be* your age or that you need to take more account of your age as limiting what you can hope to do or achieve. The sad fact is that age has been forced into being intrinsic to every relationship and to almost every judgement that people make of each other. It therefore obstructs the fullness of relationships between people by making age of the essence where it does not need to be. People are not taken as they are but according to how old they are judged to be. It is because we believe this is narrowing to the human spirit that we are proposing a new negative freedom – freedom from a kind of interference which stops people behaving more fully in accord with that part of themselves which does not change with age. The freedom from enumeration could allow a large extension of positive freedom as well. The young and the old – with unnecessary barriers removed – would be able to join the mainstream of society and leave behind the segregation which has been forced upon them.

We are arguing that the need to bring social ageing and biological ageing more into line with each other is going to become more and more pressing, even explosive. We have suffered from a cultural lag on a vast scale, and this can now only be dealt with by reducing the number of dependants in each of the age classes. The demand for a change will mount amongst the old and the young and what will eventually make it irresistible is that they will be joined by the people in the middle. For these are the people who pay the taxes which finance both the educational system for the young and the pensions for the old, and at the same time have to support their own children through their education and, sometimes, also add to what the State does for their own parents and grandparents. The burden is already substantial. There are about twenty-eight million people in the labour-force. The numbers of dependants are now almost as great if to children under sixteen are added those in further and higher education and those at the other end of life who have retired. On present trends there will soon be more dependants than there are people to depend upon. Such a state of affairs cannot continue for much longer.

Industrialisation, and the measurement of people in one dimension after another which accompanied the new technology, produced the age specialisation we described in Chapter 1. But what we are saying is that this specialisation is no longer appropriate now that older people are living so much longer than they once did and adulthood comes to younger people so much earlier than it did. Neither younger nor older any longer fit the stereotypes of childhood and old age which social control imposed. People are ready for the next big shift in society, the generation shift, to follow on the gender shift. The stage is being set for a new social contract in which less of people's individuality is surrendered to the collective.

We have followed to what seems a logical conclusion the implications of the position we have adopted throughout this book, and not just as a thought experiment. If we are right, more people of all ages will, through the institutions of the third age and in other ways as well, declare themselves against ageism. We expect that more and more of them, to take one example, will refuse to state their age in person or on official forms unless it is absolutely necessary. Every such gesture will bring a little nearer the day when the reform just proposed could become fully fledged and operational. But we have to recognise that any general transformation of attitudes and practices will not come about quickly. We are thinking more of decades than parliaments, and in some respects more of centuries than decades. In these circumstances what is necessary is to take some of the first steps which will lead in the direction of the general goal and are worthwhile in themselves even if they do not lead right up to it.

In advocating the eventual dismantling of age-stratification, we are proposing the removal of a major element in the time-structure of societies and individuals as it has prevailed so far. We could not do so unless there had already emerged from the toils of the industrial revolution a new man and a new woman who acquire a range of adult capacities earlier in life and retain them later. But one has to ask whether this new man and new woman could stand up to such a crucial abandonment. Without the modern structuring of the life-cycle into age-classes, would both the social and the psychic order be undermined? The issue will be a major one in the new time-politics which will take its place alongside physical-resource-politics in the next century.

The question has to be asked because we have put so much weight on the need for an orderly time-structure within the day, the week, the year. Within these intervals, positive liberty depends upon having boundaries. Why not also within the life? Is there not the same need for habits and breaks from habits during the course of a life? Yes, we think there is. If everything went on the same from one year to another, as people got older a great deal of life-enhancing variety would be lost. Our case is not against that but against the age-homogeneity which is imposed on individuals by society, and by the State within it. The imposition obscures individual differences; it forces people into moulds into which they would never fit on their own without being cut and trimmed. Our case is against the arrogant regimentation and homogenisation of it. It is not against, it is for people devising their own divisions within their own life-cycles, their own rhythms which correspond to their own natures. There are bound to be social conventions about how this is done. People have to live together, but they can live together without being anywhere near as rigidly lock-stepped by age as they have been forced to become. People did not obviously suffer from psychological malaise on this score before the industrial revolution, and do not in contemporary societies which have managed without taking age-stratification as far. We expect that the upshot of casting it off would be the opposite: put age down and people would flourish rather than be bowled over by the heterogeneity. The gift of time could be a gift indeed.

An ageless society

In the context of this book one implication of our main proposal has to be mentioned explicitly before we finish. If age is to be stressed less and less, is the third age to be diminished too? The answer has to be yes, eventually. But in the shorter term the third age can be one of the means by which our society in general is transformed, with older people helping to bring more plural values into the second age and with old and young and all in-between combining paid work with unpaid, and with no work, in new patterns not yet conceived. The common interest of older people, as it becomes more overt, does not need to be exclusive. It can be inclusive; it can be enlarged to include mutual solidarity and comprehensibility across the whole of society. It can be almost as much concerned with the whole as with the one segment. This will be shown by how far, in the small but vital particulars of life, older people recognise and discharge their duty to the younger as well as by the extent to which the older are holding out a different model to the rest. The younger Marx, with Engels, long ago set out a manifesto for a 'communist society' which could be one for today's third age.

As soon as the distribution of labour comes into being, each man has a particular, exclusive sphere of activity, which is forced upon him and from which he cannot escape. He is a hunter, a fisherman, a shepherd, or a critical critic, and must remain so if he does not want to lose his means of livelihood; while in communist society, where nobody has one exclusive sphere of activity but each can become accomplished in any branch he wishes, society regulates the general production and thus makes it possible for me to do one thing today and another tomorrow, to hunt in the morning, fish in the afternoon, rear cattle in the evening, criticise after dinner, just as I have a mind, without ever becoming hunter, fisherman, shepherd or critic.*

If anything like that became even more the general practice of the third age than it is now, the influence on society generally could be profound. People who had been very much full-time workers could respond by themselves striving for a better balance between, and a blurring of the edges between, work, leisure and education. There could surely be a general loosening up of the social structure if the rigidities that have been introduced into it by age were much relaxed. Education would be for people of any age instead of being so much concentrated on the first period of life; so would work instead of being reserved for the middle; and so would leisure instead of being so much the preserve of the old. Perhaps the most objectionable feature of the age-stratified society is that leisure is bestowed to such an extent – more than many people want – on the two extreme age-classes. The beneficiaries have no choice about it. They cannot take their leisure in the blocks they would like but have to follow convention. A survey reported in *The Symmetrical Family* asked people whether they would like a 'lifetime holiday' or sabbatical leave of three months or more instead of extra annual holidays, and even with that proviso many people did, with long-distance travel being what most people wanted to do with their families, sometimes while their children were still young. Further education was another draw. If leisure in mid-life were to be an alternative to leisure later, the former could be overwhelmingly popular. Once things started to shift people might

* K. Marx and F. Engels, *The German Ideology*, pp.37–8.

look back on the twentieth century as a period of almost unimaginable rigidity.

The conventional split could not indefinitely survive the new pattern we are envisaging for the third age in the new age. Their different way of life, less specialised and more fulfilling, less strained and more creative, less busy and more contemplative, could not fail to have an effect on the rest. If it also becomes more common for grandparents to play a large part in bringing up the grandchildren (and the great-grandparents too where they can) wherever the parents are disinclined or unable to do so, that could become a major influence too. As marriage becomes more fragile, the alternate generations may form new kinds of family without the actual parents taking much part in it, offering more stability to children in their formative years than many get today.

Thus the boundaries of the third age and the rest could become more blurred. The militancy could give way to something more relaxed. Those who have most to gain from softening the age categories could lead the way, after all, to a new order in which age mattered a great deal less than it has been required to so far in an age-bound society kept that way by the whip of the State.

Our focus has been on the young old. But we could catch some glimpses of what it might be like for even older people from some of our informants. Miss Prendergast said that the best moment in her day was when the afternoon sun at a certain hour shone straight into her conservatory and made its slow progress out again. She had never noticed it before she gave up her paid work and until she herself began to 'slow up'. She was a reminder that, as a contrast to activity, enjoyment of the costless pleasures has a special depth to it and many of them derive from the natural rhythms of which we are a part. There can be joy as well as sadness for the man who sweeps up the autumn leaves in Greenwich Park as well as for those who observe him, and it can intensify the same joy and sadness when that particular day comes to its end. Each day, like each year, and each life, is a reproduction of all existence, with its own spectacular beginning and its own spectacular end.

The time-structure may change. The contrasts may be played out to a different, slower, grander rhythm, with the long sweep of life back to childhood being contrasted with, and reproduced within, the day. The day at a time is more to be savoured; the day can become more vivid against the background of a life with a pattern to it, like that of Mrs Bright who wanted to use her brains for her hobbies. The older people become, the more keenly they look back, as the Ford workers looked back, to their first jobs as youngsters. But it is perhaps one of the gifts they have from nature, by no means wholly to be regretted as tragic, that their memory of recent events becomes poorer, leaving more room for the more distant. For if there is blurring of the recent, even whole spans of the recent, the more distant past of childhood and growing up can become more vivid. The one may be partly the consequence of the other. It helps the memoriser to find a sense, meaning, pattern, not just in part but in the whole of life. It is a gentle recapitulation; it can be a happy coda, not in a minor key, and a mood that can be savoured at any age.

*   *   *

We are aware – how could we not be? – that the book has been hopeful, perhaps over-hopeful, about older people who are often enough decried, ridiculed or pitied. Can old men tottering to the supermarket in their caps and their scarves bound tightly against the cold really be the harbingers of the future? Can old ladies heavy-breathing up the stairs to yet another pensioners' lunch club be the panting pathfinders? Can the obsessional gambler or greyhound breeder or butterfly collector or metal-worker making candle snuffers for the church really be in any sense pointing the way? We have given our answer and can now do no more than reiterate it.

Older people (we have been saying) have a future which is only distinct in one vital respect from the future of other people in the society to which we all belong. We are unlike in not being able to share so much of the future as it moves backwards into the continuing present, the same in being able to imagine a common future (even if it does not include us) well into the next century and beyond. The particular future we have been trying to feature is one in which positive liberty, for people of all ages, will be much more fully attained than it has been at any time since the industrial revolution.

It is difficult not to cavil at the price that people have had to pay for being relieved of a good deal of the toil, a good deal of the physical privation, a good deal of the insecurity and, above all, the early deaths which our ancestors had to endure when they were so much more dependent upon nature than we appear to be. We have given up something of that dependence but substituted another set of dependencies, upon the machines that have taken so much of the interest as well as the labour out of the work that we do, and upon the organisations that employ them and us, feed us, water us, educate us, amuse us, transport us, mimic us but always without being us. Simone Weil who worked in factories in France to study conditions in them said:

> If, in fact, the human collectivity has to a large extent freed itself from the crushing burden which the gigantic forces of nature place on frail humanity, it has, on the other hand, taken in some sort nature's place to the point of crushing the individual in a similar manner ... At last we seem to have reached that epoch predicted by Descartes when men would use 'the force and actions of fire, water, air, the stars and all the other bodies' in the same way as they do the artisans' tools, and would thus make themselves masters of nature. But, by a strange inversion, this collective dominion transforms itself into servitude as soon as one descends to the scale of the individual, and into a servitude fairly closely resembling that associated with primitive conditions of existence.*

We have picked on one particular element in the new servitude, the control over time, because we think it is as vital as it is customarily neglected in discussions of what might be, in contrast with what is. Locke said that property was an extension of the person who owned it, contained within a kind of fence which surrounded him. Time is much closer than that; it is not an extension of the person, it is part of the person; 'time is a

* S. Weil, *Oppression and Liberty* (London: Ark Paperbacks, 1988), p.79.

condition a priori', Kant said, 'of all phenomena whatsoever'.*
Someone whose time is not their own has therefore been deprived
of something much more intrinsic than property, and yet it has
not by and large been resisted nearly so strongly. So much of
people's time has been handed over to organisations which on
an unprecedented scale require the timetables of millions upon
millions of people to be synchronised with the utmost precision.
A city is a giant clock which all its citizens have to obey. Not
only does a Royal Gateman have to open the Royal Gates at
precise times; from one end of the city to another people creep
out of their homes at the same minute every morning and roll
off to their work-station or their consumer station and dead on
time go through a hundred regular motions with a thousand
others and yet are under an illusion – which cannot surely remain
intact for ever – that they are free people. Free will has been a
fiction in which society has to persuade people to believe. The
organisations which are the time controllers

> trade on a fundamental amenability. If people are told they
> have to start work at eight o'clock or secondary school at
> the age of eleven, or are to have the same length of working
> day in summer as in winter, they ordinarily obey rather
> than cavil. The common temporal framework of society
> rests upon a consent that hardly has to be asked for.**

And yet the idea of positive liberty, not always expressed in
those terms, remains as powerful an ideal as ever. It has become
more, not less attractive, to feel 'I wish to be somebody, not
nobody; a doer – deciding, not being decided for'.

It may still seem droll to cast the old, along with the young,
in the role of pioneers who have the chance to crumble the cake
of custom and strike out for a kind of liberty which is no more
agreeable than any new liberty ever is to the established order to
which we all belong. But the new facts of demography cannot be
brushed aside nor the rigidities of an industry which has shown

* I. Kant, *Critique of Pure Reason* (London: Dent, 1956), p.47.
** M. Young, *The Metronomic Society – Natural Rhythms and Human Time-tables*, p.229.

itself (except when pushed by labour-shortages) unwilling to employ either the 'old' or the 'young' on any scale. At each end of the life cycle people have had one kind of negative freedom thrust upon them, and the potential consequences for the rest of society cannot be lightly dismissed. The young have made a bid, and could make it a more powerful one if they would consider more comprehensively the whole of the house, rather than only the room, to which they have been invited and invited each other.

So it is with older people if they too emphasise as much what they have to contribute to the whole as to gain from it. They can – some of them have begun to – create their own structures around lives more free than they ever had while they were solely workers. We have seen how large a task it is to break away even partially from the habits of a working lifetime, and how hard to acknowledge, without overdoing it, that people cannot do without a time-structure even though it is in some part their own to make. It would be expecting too much for third agers to have yet made much of a dent on the general ethos. They live in a society which has been dominated by ordinary work and it has not been, and will not be, easy to break free from that domination. In a society like ours leisure partakes of the character of work, and we can hardly imagine what it would be like if it did not and expectations of the good life began to shift over to a new pattern. We do not pretend that third agers, any more than anyone else, have yet done this or appreciated the opportunities of positive liberty as much as they could. A society in which they make use of their potential is still a potential even if they have begun to stir themselves.

This new society will not readily come from the multitudes of ordinary working people who are more or less happily bound into the habits of their workplaces, the habits of believing that the only respectable state for older people is retirement from a job that gave them their purpose in life, the habits of a consumer society and the habits which persuade them that affluence, however strange some of its manifestations, is the proper reward for the effort they make to be punctual and to act punctually according to the orders they are given or give themselves. But it could come from the older and younger people who are not under quite the same mundane pressures and, if it does, that could gradually shift the whole society away from its acquisitive tread-mill which keeps people poor by raising their expectations of what they should have as fast as (or faster than) they add to what they actually have. The stage is being set for a retreat from mass society and for greater variety, greater idiosyncrasy, greater individuality and perhaps greater fulfilment.

In all this we are saying that the kind of positive liberty we are envisaging for one age group is compatible with such liberty in general. We have not been asking just for the sake of paradox that older people be more fully their own masters (and so more fully individual, more idiosyncratic) and simultaneously more fully younger people's servants. Affection descends more readily than it ascends – that seems to be a fact of life. But so should duties descend more readily as long as older people are hale and capable as much of giving as receiving. It would be a thin conception of liberty that concentrated only on the liberties of individuals of any age as though they were not also members of the wider all-age society from which they both derive their liber-ties and their duties to respect and enhance the liberties of others. Positive liberty and the confidence to use it by those in the third age should imply a commitment to the positive liberty of others, and especially of those in the first age. This is intrinsic to any argument which views an age-group not just as a mini-society but as a part of society which could still have some independent influence on the whole. This could happen as we move into a future less dominated by work which is, except in a financial sense, signally unrewarding.

Virginia Woolf wrote of the gift of her own talent and how she was allowed to express it, freed from the necessity

> always to be doing work that one did not wish to do, and to do it like a slave, flattering and fawning, not always necessarily perhaps, but it seemed necessary and the stakes were too high to run risks; and then thought of that one gift which it was death to hide – a small one but dear to the possessor – perishing and with it myself, my soul – all this became like a rust eating away the bloom of the spring.*

* V. Woolf, *A Room of One's Own* (London: Chatto & Windus, 1954), p.38.

The Third Age as a Term

In the way we have used the term we have parted company from Laslett (whom we quoted in Chapter 1) and from most other people who have defined the third age by marking it off not just from an age that came before but from an age that comes after. Laslett and others distinguish it from a fourth age which is an 'era of final dependence, decrepitude and death'.*

The main part of the case for a fourth age as well as a third is that it burnishes up the latter by tarnishing the former. The fourth can be seen as the age of *the* old, and the third kept for those who have not yet arrived there. Instead of having to think of hale and hearty fifty and sixty and seventy-year-olds who have left work as old, they can be thought of as something else, intermediate, on the way but not yet old, avoiding all the unfortunate associations which go with the tarnishing word.

This obstinate unwillingness to see the Third Age apart from the Fourth has sanctioned their exclusion from activities, especially earning activities, for which nearly all of them have been perfectly well suited, has debased their status in the eyes of their juniors, and above all has devalued them in their own estimation of themselves.'**

But elevating the third by the comparison is only done by treading down the fourth. The labelling problem is wished on to even older and more defenceless people.*** Peter is robbed to

* P. Laslett, *A Fresh Map of Life*, p.4.
** Laslett, p.5.
*** Professor Margot Jefferys first convinced us that the 'fourth age' is a concept which should be dropped.

pay Paul, even though Peter is already poorer. The objection, which we think insuperable, is that if 'true' old age is taken to be something beyond the third age 'the very old are distanced from society more than ever'.*

As people age in all the ways that body and mind are heir to, many of them do in fact end their lives in a state of dependence which goes well beyond financial dependence, in old people's homes, in geriatric hospitals or, more often, in their own homes being cared for by their own families. But that alone does not justify marking off a separate age of dependency and decrepitude as if it were as inevitable as growing up, and certainly not doing so primarily in order to beef up the morale of the already relatively beefy. For many young people are sufficiently handicapped to be dependent in the same way, while many old people die without ever being in that state and still more would never be if more help was given to them to stay out of it. The goal is a long life and a quick death (as we said in Chapter 1) and it is at least possible that the current obsession of younger people with their health will deliver them into old age even better equipped to avoid, or hold off, decrepitude. In adopting this approach we recognise that we are taking a basically optimistic line on a contentious subject – believing that better medicine and better standards generally are going to allow ever more people to stay healthy almost to the end – rather than the opposite, basically pessimistic line, that better medicine and better standards are going to keep more people alive with poorer health. We prefer the wholly optimistic to the half-optimistic of the people who are optimistic about the third age only to collapse into extreme pessimism about what follows it.

For us, the clinching argument came from our own survey. We had in our sample several people in their fifties and early sixties who were in some degree disabled. They came into our account in Chapter 4. Disabled they might be, but this did not mean they were notably dependent and certainly did not mean that they were decrepit. We could not label them fourth age. Some of them were not so at all. Miss Prendergast was definitely among the most positive of third agers. We could not count her,

* F. Cribier, 'Changes in Life Course and Retirement in Recent Years', p.200.

or the others, as fourth age. Even if people became more dependent upon others for physical support they could still find much worthwhile to live for. Another survey of the elderly, in Devon, found that 'people with apparently severe handicaps' had a 'remarkable capacity . . . to adapt to their situation and cope with it cheerfully'.* Why should people with such capacities not remain in the third age? Why should the third age be made more brilliant by contrasting it with another stage certainly not brilliant and not necessarily inevitable?

* R.A.B. Leaper, *Age Speaks for Itself*, p.62.

The Place and the Sample

Our intentions were general and ambitious. We had to do more than just exchange our thoughts with each other. We needed to discuss them with others chosen with an element of randomness. Our quarry was likely to be elusive. Being concerned as we were (and are) with people's state of mind as well as their apparently objective circumstances, we knew we had to concentrate on a few people about whom we might be able to find a good deal rather than spreading ourselves over many; and if, for convenience, we were going to confine ourselves to relatively few people they might as well be in one place. We knew in any case that we would not be able to generalise even about our chosen district, Greenwich, and certainly not about 'old' people there since our informants were not old at all as judged by some criteria. But we did not count this a great disadvantage. We hoped for guidance about a series of dilemmas and this could come from a single individual as well as from a collection of them.

We chose Greenwich partly because it was the site of another study not altogether dissimilar from ours, made in the 1930s. The student was then Professor E. Wight Bakke who had come to South London from Yale University.* He also gave us advice when the Institute of Community Studies was first set up on our side of the Thames. His was not a study of retirement but of unemployment (although many older people were unemployed before 'early retirement' was in vogue) and, to find out about it, he interviewed 161 unemployed men (no women) and also many others with views to pass on to him. He supplemented his talks by moving about on foot and looking around him from the tops

---

* See E. Wight Bakke, *The Unemployed Man – a Social Study.*

of the trams to which he seemed to be devoted, noting what he saw as they trundled backwards and forwards from one end to another of this 'long and narrow borough'. He was obsessed with people standing around doing 'nothing'. For two months he went the length of the waterfront by tram at 'peak loafing times' and walked back on foot, all the while diligently counting the number of loafers he could see. On an average day he could count 260 of them. But there was always a cluster of people waiting around to enter the Labour Exchange, and since they were, if loafing at all, not doing so from choice, he deducted them from the total. This brought his number of loafers down to 210. The number seemed pleasingly low.

He sat so indefatigably on the top of trams and walked about as indefatigably because his hope was the opposite of ours, perhaps in its own very small way itself a sign of the times in both periods. He hoped that in Greenwich the work ethic had not been undermined. People who got money for not working might not want to work at all. They might be content to loaf or, just as bad, gamble. He was told by a licensed riverman, in a trade which was highly active when Shakespeare was playing *As You Like It* in South London, but which was already in steep decline and has now almost disappeared:

> You've seen that lot in front of St Alfege's, haven't you? Well, they spend the whole day doing just one thing. From the time they get there in the morning, till the noon edition comes out, they discuss the chances of the horses or dogs they are going to back. Home for dinner. Back again and keep track of the winners as they come in. Home for tea. Then back in the evening to boast about or excuse their luck till nine-thirty or ten.*

But despite the censorious riverman, Bakke went back to America a happy man, concluding that the work ethic was very much alive on this side of the Atlantic. 'The behaviour of the unemployed in searching for new employment gives no evidence that the possibility of drawing Unemployment Insurance Benefit

* Bakke, p.189.

has retarded the efforts of the unemployed to get back to work.'*
He was comforted by the fact that his 210 loafers were only 8%
of the registered unemployed in the borough. The rest (as he
found in his interviews) were 'not idling their time away' but,
although he rather surprisingly regretted they were not reading
more books on the social sciences, they were at least engaged in
highly useful tasks at home or visiting the cinema, often with
the whole family.

> Weekend parties in which the whole family occupies a 'pew'
> in the local picture house are common. The influence of
> these hours extends far beyond the time spent in the theatre.
> There is food for conversation both in anticipation of the
> next show and in the thoughts of the ones attended weeks
> and months ago.**

This was a thoroughly wholesome occupation for the hours not
spent looking for work and one not available at Marienthal
(mentioned in Chapter 1) where there was no cinema. In the
shadow of Wren's Observatory all was not too desperate as long
as the unemployed were in the cinema with their wives and their
children enjoying the latest film from Hollywood. Would he have
thought the same today about them 'pounding the box', as one
of our informants said her family spent the winter in doing?

We chose Greenwich, as well as for Bakke, because there
seemed to be some symbolic appropriateness in it for a study in
time-sociology and it is near to our base at the Institute of
Community Studies in Bethnal Green, just over the water, or
under the river Thames by the Blackwall and Rotherhithe Tun-
nels. In Greenwich the past is very much present. The Dover
Road to which the Blackwall Tunnel gives access is an old
Roman road which crosses the borough. The Greenwich Observatory which stands on the hill in Greenwich Park is on the
Meridian which is still the benchmark for all the billions of
clocks in the world. They are all in phased unison with GMT.
On the outside of Christopher Wren's Observatory Tower a ball

* Bakke, p.143.
** Bakke, pp.178-9.

still drops down at exactly 1 p.m. every day to indicate just what the time is. But this visible manifestation of the present moment is now pointless, except in so far as it draws attention to a past when London was far and away the largest port in the world and tens of thousands of shipmasters crowded the waters of the Pool of London. Before sailing, they set their chronometers by eye, training their telescopes on the ball to register the exact moment of its fall. The shipmasters have now gone. Only an occasional tugboat chugs past with its convoy of barges laden with oil from the Gulf or liquid gas from Algeria for the power stations or gasometers further up the river. But the past, visually vivid, lives on, in Sweet Thames itself, which is the northern boundary of the borough; in the Palace of Greenwich which lies resplendent and stately by the side of it, palace still in grandeur though not in use; in the National Maritime Museum, and in the historic tea-clipper, the Cutty Sark, which is now literally set in concrete by Greenwich pier.

The Park, the Observatory, the Palace and the clipper are in old Greenwich. The modern borough of that name also includes what was until the amalgamation of 1965 the separate borough of Woolwich. Woolwich was for long almost as famous for its Royal Arsenal, at least inside the Kingdom, as Greenwich has been for its Observatory. As the official obituary of Woolwich put it, 'throughout the centuries the prosperity of Woolwich has depended on war and rumour of war'.* The old Greenwich strip, a rather narrow strip alongside the river, has now been enlarged by this other area which bulges out across the drained marshland of Thamesmead and reaches as far inland as Eltham. Woolwich has more council housing than Greenwich, with many tower blocks overlooking docks no longer used for their original purpose.

As for our sample within Greenwich, we have already said in Chapter 1 that our sample consisted of men between fifty and the official pensionable age of sixty-five, and of women between fifty and their official pensionable age of sixty. They had all for whatever reason left full-time employment within the previous

* E.F.E. Jefferson, *The Woolwich Story 1890–1965* (Woolwich District Antiquarian Society, 1970), p.41.

two years. We should now say how we found them. Such people are not easy to find. What we did was to enlist the help of General Practitioners who as doctors in the National Health Service have pretty well comprehensive lists of people enumerated by age. The Professor of General Practice at Guy's Hospital, which is just outside the borough, introduced us to five GPs who had practices which between them reflected the diverse social mix of Greenwich. We are grateful to all of them for their help. We drew from their lists the names of all the people they had within the age spans we had decided upon, 3,161 of them in all.

The GP records did not show which of these people had left paid work. So we sent the 3,161 a questionnaire asking them for some basic information about themselves; those who did not at once reply were sent a reminder. The overall response rate was 76%. Out of these, 192 people satisfied our conditions and 149 of them agreed to be interviewed. We asked them subsequently to fill in a diary showing how long they spent on various activities quarter of an hour by quarter of an hour over two weekdays. We interviewed some of the people several times.

Given our resources we could not include more GPs and draw a larger sample. What we hoped to do was to see the members of the sample as individuals in order to stimulate reflection, suggest hypotheses and ideas, generate hints from a person here and there about the questions we should be asking about life in later years which could, if they were interesting enough, be tested out elsewhere with larger samples, for larger areas and with people who *are* already older. Moreover, to provide the right kind of stimulus as well as interviews a good deal of observation would be needed (though not from the tops of trams), since what people do is not necessarily the same as what they say they do. The sample was not large enough in size to be representative and we cannot claim statistical significance for the kind of findings we have presented. Even if the sample had been a good deal larger, people of this age who had left paid work in the last two years were an unusual group, a minority, and certainly not representative of their age-group as a whole, let alone the population generally in Greenwich. We also chose two other groups which are certainly not representative either – workers who were moving into retirement from a car factory and a local hospital.

The bulk of the interviewing was done in 1984 and 1985, with some follow-up interviews being done in later years. The first book to result developed a framework for looking at the Greenwich results: Michael Young's *The Metronomic Society*. The 'theory' of time-sociology behind the present book was contained in that one. We have no way of knowing how different our impressions would have been had we done the interviews later in our lives and in the century, only that the impressions would certainly have been different – if only because there was relatively heavy unemployment at the time and older people were particularly vulnerable to it, although this incidence and vulnerability persisted as a stubborn fact throughout the subsequent upswing. Our conclusions would also have been different if we had given ourselves less time to ponder them and to fill out a wider context in which to place the study.

Select Bibliography

Arber, S. and Gilbert, N. 'Transitions in Caring: gender, life course and the care of the elderly' in B. Bytheway et al. (eds), *Being and Becoming Old*, London, Sage, 1989, pp.72–92.

Armstrong, P. *Technical Change and Reductions in Life Hours of Work*, London, Technical Change Centre, 1984.

Bakke, E. Wight. *The Unemployed Man – a social study*, London, Nisbet, 1933.

Beauvoir, S. de. *Old Age*, London, André Deutsch, 1972.

Bengston, V.L. 'Sociological Perspectives on Ageing, Families and the Future' in M. Bergener, M. Ermini and H. Stahelin (eds), *Dimensions in Ageing*, London, Academic Press, 1986.

Berlin, I. *Four Essays on Liberty*, Oxford University Press, 1988.

Blythe, R. *Akenfield*, London, Allen Lane, 1969.

—— *The View in Winter*, Harmondsworth, Penguin, 1981.

Burrow, J.A. *The Ages of Man*, Oxford, Clarendon Press, 1986.

Carroll, P. *Pension Age in a Changing Society*, London, Pensions and Population Research Institute, 1989.

Casey, B. and Laczko, F. 'Early Retired or Long-Term Unemployed' *Work, Employment and Society* 3:4 (1989), pp.509–27.

Chudacoff, H. *How Old Are You? Age Consciousness in American Culture*, New Jersey, Princeton University Press, 1989.

Cribier, F. 'Changes in Life Course and Retirement in Recent Years' in P. Johnson, C. Conrad and D. Thomson (eds), *Workers versus Pensioners*, Manchester University Press, 1989.

Dale, A. and Bamford, C. 'Older Workers and the Peripheral Workforce: the Erosion of Gender Differences', *Ageing and Society* 8, 1988, pp.43–62.

Daniel, W.W. 'Whatever Happened to the Workers in Woolwich?', London, Political and Economic Planning, 1972, *Planning*, Vol.XXXVIII, Broadsheet 537.

Davies, K. *Women and Time: Weaving the Strands of Everyday Life*, University of Lund, 1989.

Durant, H. *The Problem of Leisure*, London, Routledge, 1938.

Fogarty, M. *Meeting the Needs of the Elderly*, Dublin, The European

SELECT BIBLIOGRAPHY

Foundation for the Improvement of Living and Working Conditions, 1987.

Fromm, E. *The Fear of Freedom*, London, Ark Paperbacks, 1984.

Gaullier, X. *La Deuxième Carrière: âges, emplois, retraités*, Paris, Seuil, 1988.

Goldthorpe, J., Lockwood, D., Bechhofer, F. and Platt, J. *The Affluent Worker in the Class Struggle*, Cambridge University Press, 1969.

Handy, C.B. *The Future of Work*, Oxford, Blackwell, 1984.

Hannah, L. *Inventing Retirement*, Cambridge University Press, 1986.

Hareven, T.K. *Family Time and Industrial Time*, Cambridge University Press, 1982.

House of Commons Employment Committee, *The Employment Patterns of the Over 50s*, 2 vols, HMSO, 1989.

Jahoda, M. *Employment and Unemployment – a Social Psychological Analysis*, Cambridge University Press, 1982.

Jahoda, M., Lazarsfeld, P. and Zeisel, H. *Marienthal: the Sociography of an Unemployed Community*, London, Tavistock, 1972.

Jolly, J., Creigh, S. and Mingay, A. *Age as a Factor in Employment*, London, Department of Employment Research Paper 11, April 1980.

Laczko, F. and Phillipson, C. 'Age Discrimination in Employment' in E. McEwen (ed.), *Age: the Unrecognised Discrimination*, London, Age Concern, 1990.

Laslett, P. *A Fresh Map of Life*, London, Weidenfeld and Nicolson, 1989.

Leaper, R.A.B. *Age Speaks for Itself*, Exeter District Health Authority, 1988.

Lindley, R.M. and Wilson, R.A. (eds) *Review of the Economy and Employment 1988–89 – Vol.1: Occupational Assessment*, Coventry, Institute for Employment Research, University of Warwick, 1989.

McKay, D.I. and Reid, G.L. 'Redundancy, Unemployment and Manpower Policy', *Economic Journal*, December 1972.

Malthus, T.R. *Principles of Political Economy*, London, John Murray, 1820 edn.

Marx, K. and Engels, F. *The German Ideology*, London, Lawrence and Wishart, 1973.

Midwinter, E. *Age is Opportunity*, London, Centre for Policy on Ageing, 1982.

—— 'Your Country Doesn't Need You!' in E. McEwen (ed.), *Age: the Unrecognised Discrimination*, London, Age Concern, 1990.

Minois, G. *History of Old Age, From Antiquity to the Renaissance*, Cambridge, Polity Press, 1989.

Morris, J. 'Three aspects of the person in social life' in R. Ruddock (ed.), *Six Approaches to the Person*, London, Routledge and Kegan Paul, 1972.

Ogburn, W.F. with Tibbins, C. 'The Family and its Functions', *Recent Trends in the United States: Report of the President's Research Committee on Social Trends*, New York, McGraw Hill, 1933.

Organisation for Economic Co-operation and Development. *Reforming Public Pensions*, Paris, OECD, 1988.

Pamuk, E.R. 'Social Class Inequality in Mortality from 1921 to 1972 in England and Wales', *Population Studies* 39:3 (March 1985), pp.17–31.

Parker, S. *Work and Retirement*, London, Allen and Unwin, 1982.

Phillipson, C. *Capitalism and the Construction of Old Age*, London, Macmillan, 1982.

Quennell, M. and C.B.B. *History of Everyday Things in England*, London, Batsford, 1941.

Schuller, T. *Education and the Third Age*, London, Education Reform Group, 1989.

Schuller, T. and Walker, A. *The Time of Our Life: Education, Employment and Retirement in the Third Age*, London, Institute for Public Policy Research, Employment Paper 2, 1990.

Sinfield, A. *The Long-term Unemployed*, Paris, OECD, 1968.

Sorokin, P. *Sociocultural Causality, Space and Time*, Durham, North Carolina, Duke University Press, 1943.

Thompson, E.P. 'Time, Work, Discipline and Industrial Capitalism', *Past and Present* 38 (1967), pp.56–97.

Thompson, P., Itzin, C. and Abendstern, M. *I Don't Feel Old – the Experience of Later Life*, Oxford University Press, 1990.

Tompkins, P. *Flexibility and Fairness – a study in equalisation of pension ages and benefits*, The Joseph Rowntree Memorial Trust, York, 1989.

Townsend, P. *The Family Life of Old People – An Inquiry in East London*, London, Routledge and Kegan Paul, 1957.

Tucker, N. *What is a Child?*, London, Open Books, 1977.

Warr, P. *Work, Unemployment and Mental Health*, Oxford, Clarendon Press, 1987.

Wilkinson, R.G. 'Class Mortality Differentials, Income Distribution and Trends in Poverty 1921–1981', *Journal of Social Policy* 18:3 (July 1989), pp.307–36.

Young, M. *The Metronomic Society – Natural Rhythms and Human Timetables*, London, Thames and Hudson, 1988.

Young, M. and Willmott, P. *The Symmetrical Family*, Harmondsworth, Penguin, 1975.

Index

INDEX

Jeffreys, Professor Margot 181n
job-leaving ceremonies 103–5, 161–2
Jolly, J. 8n
Journal en miettes 96n

Kant, I. 178, 178n
Kundera, Milan 25n

labour force v. number of dependants 171
labour market, convergence of men and
    women in 130–6
Laczko, F. 61n, 157n
Laslett, P. 18n, 19, 19n, 158n, 160, 160n,
    181n
Leaper, R. A. B. 183
leisure
    age-stratified society and 174
    choices regarding 174
    compulsory, spoiled by lack of money
    69
Leverhulme Trust 24
Liberty, negative and positive sense of 20,
    21–4, 101–2, 105–13, 176–80
    see also freedom *and* third age
life-cycles, segmentation of 9
life expectancy, improvement in 10
Lindley, R. M. 153n
'*L'Insertion Sociale des Préretraites*' 76n
Locke, John 177
Lockwood, D. 48n
Long-Term Unemployed, The 87n

McKay, D. I. 87n
Malthus, T. R. 5, 5n
Mandela, Nelson 116
manual workers
    in car factory, insecurity of 30
    early ageing in 37–8
Marienthal, M. Jahoda's study of
    unemployed people 23–4, 120, 121,
    136n, 187
*Marienthal: The Sociography of an
    Unemployed Community* 24n, 136,
    136n
Marx, K. 173–4, 174n
medical retirement 70–75, 92, 110,
    111–13, 182–3
Meer, F. 116n
Meeting the Needs of the Elderly 150n,
    160n
memory, fading of the, with age 114–15
Metronomic Society, The 23, 178n
Midwinter, Eric 157n, 160n
Mingay, A. 8n
Minois, G. 2n
Mobility Allowance 111, 112

Morris, John 95n
mortality differentials between social
    classes 85–6
motability 112

National Dividend, concept of 167–8
nightwork, human cost of 36–7, 54–5
'normal' retirement, acceptance/
    non-acceptance of 79–81

Ogburn, William 5n
Old Age 8on, 96n
older people
    future of 176
    merits of, for employment 154n
    re-employment, difficulty in obtaining
    62–6
    removal from labour force 5–6, 8
'Older Workers and the Peripheral
    Workforce: The Erosion of Gender
    Differences' 131n
Open College of the Arts 161
Open University 161
Oppression and Liberty 177n
Organisation for Economic Co-operation
    and Development 10n
over-seventy-five age group, growth in 10

paid v. unpaid work 151
Pamuk, E. R. 86n
parasuicide 123n
Parker, S. 76n
Parkes, C. M. 132n
pension age
    common retirement age, private sector
    158–9
    for State pension 152–6
    women 158
Pension Age in the Changing Society 159n
Pensioner Premium, concept of a 155
pets as time-structure setters 118
Phillipson, C. 154n, 157n
Plato 21–2n
Platt, J. 48n
polarisation, social 85–8
population, proportion of pensionable
    age 10
pre-industrial society
    employment of children 2–3
    the family in 2–3
Principles of Political Economy 5n
Principles of Psychology, The 113n, 114n
private domain, placing the age of adults
    in the 166
private occupational pension schemes,
    common retirement ages 158–9

196